MIMETIC THEORY AND BIBLICAL INTERPRETATION

CASCADE COMPANIONS

The Christian theological tradition provides an embarrassment of riches: from Scripture to modern scholarship, we are blessed with a vast and complex theological inheritance. And yet this feast of traditional riches is too frequently inaccessible to the general reader.

The Cascade Companions series addresses the challenge by publishing books that combine academic rigor with broad appeal and readability. They aim to introduce nonspecialist readers to that vital storehouse of authors, documents, themes, histories, arguments, and movements that comprise this heritage with brief yet compelling volumes.

RECENT TITLES IN THIS SERIES:

MIMETIC THEORY AND BIBLICAL INTERPRETATION

Reclaiming the Good News of the Gospel

MICHAEL HARDIN

CASCADE *Books* • Eugene, Oregon

MIMETIC THEORY AND BIBLICAL INTERPRETATION
Reclaiming the Good News of the Gospel

Cascade Companions

Cascade Books
An Imprint of Wipf and Stock Publishers
199 W. 8th Ave., Suite 3
Eugene, OR 97401

www.wipfandstock.com

PAPERBACK ISBN: 978-1-5326-0110-1
HARDCOVER ISBN: 978-1-5326-0112-5
EBOOK ISBN: 978-1-5326-0111-8

Cataloguing-in-Publication data:

Names: Hardin, Michael.

Title: Mimetic Theory and Biblical Interpretation : Reclaiming the Good News of the Gospel / Michael Hardin.

Description: Eugene, OR: Cascade Books, 2017 | Series: Cascade Companions | Includes bibliographical references.

Identifiers: ISBN 978-1-5326-0110-1 (paperback) | ISBN 978-1-5326-0112-5 (hardcover) | ISBN 978-1-5326-0111-8 (ebook)

Subjects: LCSH: Girard, Rene, 1923–2015—Criticism and interpretation. | Mimesis in the Bible.

Classification: LCC BL65.V55 H2 2017 (print) | LCC BL65.V55 (ebook)

Manufactured in the U.S.A.   06/14/17

In Memoriam
Raymund Schwager

"Here is a genuine Israelite in
whom there is no deceit."

CONTENTS

ACKNOWLEDGMENTS

I ALWAYS ENJOY WRITING on René Girard and mimetic theory. More so, I have always enjoyed teaching mimetic theory in seminars, conferences, in churches, colleges and seminaries. While the explosion of sociological approaches to the Bible have proliferated like rabbits and scholars have much better understandings of the real world of Second Temple Judaism than they did a generation ago, there is still the need for a tool by which both academic and non-academic can approach the biblical text. The gap between the academy and the church must be bridged and perhaps our generation can help build those bridges. While hyper-intellectualism is certainly overrated, for too long Christianity in America has suffered under the illusion that anti-intellectualism is a spiritual gift and that ignorance is a theological virtue. A Christianity that does not "love the Lord God . . . with her mind" is a pseudo-Christianity.

Acknowledgments

First, thanks are proffered to Christian Amondson for inviting me to write this primer for Cascade. Brian Palmer graciously tolerated my delays and was very gentle in his encouragements bringing this text to publication and thanks to Mary Roth for carefully tending to my manuscript and clarifying it in any number of ways! As always I am grateful to my wife Lorri who listened to me read this to her as we drove from Pennsylvania to Michigan and made many suggestions for improving the manuscript. I am especially grateful to my friend Jonathan Sauder who has, in the midst of his own studies, taken the time to read and comment on the manuscript. He has not just clarified the text but has also made his own contributions.

I will forever be grateful to Fr. Raymund Schwager for introducing me to the work of René Girard. His untimely death in 2004 was a huge loss not only to mimetic theorists but also to the Church. It is an honor to dedicate this book to his beautiful memory.

Michael Hardin
Lancaster, PA
Pentecost 2016

1

PRELUDE

The Republican National Convention of 2016 begins today in Cleveland. Just this past month, we saw any number of unarmed or legally armed black men killed by police, while police in Dallas and Baton Rouge were assassinated. Turkey managed to shrug off a coup, the United States and her allies are squaring off with China in the Pacific Rim, and the counter-terror efforts against ISIS still continues in Iraq and Syria. It feels like the world is about to explode. Why? What is the origin of this sense of doom that hangs like a pall over our collective destiny?

We can add to this the economic malaise we see globally. You may be thinking, "But Michael, they are talking about the DOW hitting 20,000, how can you talk about malaise?" When less than one hundred people have a net worth that combined is greater than that of the bottom 50 percent in the world, all I can say is "Houston, we have a problem." The middle class in America is barely hanging on; poverty levels continue to increase in what is supposed to be the world's greatest superpower. Why do the rich get richer and the poor get poorer? Why do celebrities and sports figures and those who appear in the media get paid exponentially more than teachers? Why do people crush one another to death for Wal-Mart Black Friday sales? Why do couples destroy once vibrant relationships? Why do human beings seek fulfillment in possessions?

This is the real world we live in. It is complex or at least it appears so as a kind of historical jigsaw puzzle whose pieces don't quite fit one another very well. I frequently hear about how reading or watching the news leaves people feeling depressed. So many things seem just unexplained or unexplainable. It is almost as if there is a determinism at work that we cannot control and to whose fate we must resign. I know these feelings well. I have three daughters and two teen-age granddaughters and I wonder what kind of future we are leaving for the next generations. You can see why I have little patience for "pie-in-the-sky-by-and-by" theologies. I have given up on a *deus ex machina,* as all authentic Christian theology has had to do following the events of the Shoah. The King in the Sky controlling all things like some divine puppet master, a god whose inscrutable will created nothing but existential angst—I rejected this kind of deity. I could not and would not put my faith in a god who had an exclusive country club whose membership was by invitation only. I refuse to place my trust in any deity that is two-faced.

I do, however, affirm the God of the Nicene Creed, which is my theological ruler. The early trinitarian baptismal creeds and later, the Nicene Creed of 325 and its revision in Constantinople in 381, have always functioned as the starting point for any Christian discussion on or about God. In other words, when I think theologically I know that if I am to do so in such a way that is to be a benefit to the church I am obliged to begin here. Later the relationship between theology and certain sciences will be made clear, but for now I am putting my cards on the table. I have a lot of questions about history, culture and religion and I believe that the Abba of Jesus is related by the Spirit to all reality.

After my crash-and-burn ministry in the early 1990s, the only way to make a living that I knew was waiting tables. I did that until I eventually went into marketing. I even worked for a short while at Dale Carnegie. One thing I learned is that sales people have techniques they use to move us toward purchasing their product. When it is done well, it is a real skill to behold. Again, remaining open and transparent, I have several questions that have as their desired intention to lead you to a certain realization.

1. Have you ever babysat children and wondered why two children in a room full of toys end up fighting over the same toy?

2. Have you ever noticed how quickly an argument escalates into a fight? Why does this happen? How does it happen?

3. Have you ever known persons who were the "black sheep" of their family system? Or have you been part of a socially marginalized group?

4. Have you noticed how people unite after tragedy strikes? Why?

5. Have you ever wondered why people lie and deceive one another? Or why we keep so many secrets? Or how those secrets and deceptions create all manner of dis-ease?

If you were able to engage these questions it is safe to say that you will understand this book and you will not only grasp mimetic theory but will be able to use it as an interpretive tool for all of life, including both texts and relationships. In other words, one does not just apply a particular hermeneutic to the biblical text and another one to one's familial relationships—perhaps, for example, the historical-critical or the allegorical to the former and a psychoanalytic or empirical one to the latter. Texts and relationships can and may be interpreted through the same lens. The mimetic theory is not in competition with other biblical interpretive methods; it can be a complement to many contemporary and ancient methods of interpretation. It is, however, a direct challenge to a number of underlying presumptions in which Christian theology finds itself embedded. These presuppositions have nothing to do with theology or doctrines of God but strictly with one's view of humanity, or anthropology. What is a human being? What does it mean to be human? Does the Bible have anything to say about "being human"? If so, what is the relationship between what exegesis might observe in the biblical text and the current results of scientific anthropology? Is it possible to bring the Bible and modern science into dialogue on this subject?

In order to facilitate our conversation let's go right for the jugular: It would appear that the view of God in the Christian scriptures is different than that found in the Jewish scriptures. How one handles that apparent difference is crucial. Almost all scholars will trace this question back to Marcion of Sinope in the second century.[1] The perception that the God of the Jewish Scriptures is retributive

1. Marcion has come back in vogue as a research topic this past decade with many groundbreaking new works on his thought and life.

is common and needs no defense. The problem arises when one seeks to juxtapose the non-retributive ethics of Jesus, whom the apostolic tradition claims revealed God, with a God who would seek to murder Moses, command genocide, demand the sacrifice of a child or visit destruction upon both cities and the planet. In the words of the Sesame Street song, "One of these things is not like the other."

Marcion handled this problem by arguing that the Jewish scriptures and the Jewish God were inferior to the Christian scriptures and the Christian God. The Jewish God was the demiurge or creator but the real, true God was pure spirit. There are two streams of revelation, one inferior and one superior. In our own time, particularly due to Jewish-Christian dialogue in biblical studies and theology, we recognize that this is not a satisfactory way to relate the two traditions. However, since the second century, the Christian tradition has also recognized this. While only a few early church fathers were in contact with Amoraic Judaism (70–200 C.E.), the Greek Septuagint was the book that the early Christians used to demonstrate that God had fulfilled the promises made by the prophets in Jesus. The problem that Marcion raised in the early second century haunted the early church and would continue to haunt Christian institutions for the next 1,900 years. In *The Jesus Driven Life*, I juxtaposed the views of Marcion and Justin Martyr on the relation of the two Testaments and concluded that they both incorrectly answered the question inasmuch as both gave supercessionist responses.

Late second century Alexandrian (and later Caesarean) catechist and commentator Origen recognized that literal, face-value historical interpretation of the

Jewish scriptures simply would not work and following the allegorical interpretive tradition of Alexandria (found also, for example, in Philo), would read the text spiritually. When the biblical text told stories of God as retributive or vengeful, the proper way to understand this was with reference to the battle within the self, between the greater mind and the lesser emotions or passions. This reading, though just as dualistic as Marcion's, had the advantage of being able to develop a "biblical theology." Even though certain of Origen's theological conclusions were condemned at the Council of Alexandria in 400 CE, allegorical interpretation would end up trumping the historical-literal reading of Antioch, and the entirety of late antique and medieval theology would tend toward an allegorical rendering of Scripture.[2] In the West, it was Augustine's allegorical hermeneutic that would provide the primary tool for engaging Scripture until the mid-1600s and the beginnings of the historical-critical method.[3]

Every commentator on the subject that I have read on the relation of the Testaments has been supercessionist from Justin Martyr to Karl Barth. To be fair, Barth is the least supercessionist, but in the end, the Christian faith is the true religion in Barth.[4] Marcion's supercessionist solution to toss the Old Testament scriptures because they were "old" has never been an option for Christian theology and the Church got sucked into asking the wrong question about the relationship of the Testaments from the get-go. As we will see, the right approach is to ask about a specific relationship occurring within these two

2. Kugel and Greer, *Early Biblical Interpretation*; Rogerson, Rowland, and Lindars, *Study and Use;* Simonetti, *Biblical Interpretation*.

3. Kummel, *Investigation*; Scholder, *Birth*.

4. Hardin, *Must God be Violent?*

collections of literature. The biblical canon as a hermeneutic problem does indeed contain a juxtaposition but it
is not the difference between the Testaments; it is a difference that is shot through both Testaments from Genesis
through Revelation.

The genius of Marcion to form a collection of sacred
apostolic writing, and the Church's subsequent need to
define that sacred collection by recognizing certain texts
as "holy," was not in itself a bad idea. We must remember
that the literature of the entire Bible, with perhaps the ex-
ception of the writer of Luke-Acts, was composed by Jews.
The whole thing is a collection of Jewish texts. A portion
of those texts was composed by Jews who followed the
Jesus tradition. Therefore the relation of the Testaments
should never be about the difference between Christians
and Jews. Rather we should be asking the question as to
what the implications of following Jesus' path were within
Judaism. If we approach the question this way then we
can begin our search for an internal biblical hermeneutic
that is contained in and spans both Testaments.

Before we do that, however, the elephant in the room
must be acknowledged: the Bible is a sacred text to most
Protestants. In Catholicism and Orthodoxy the biblical
text is sacred only in the sense that it is the primary witness to that which the church believes and acts in her divine worship. Revelation, or God's word, comes through
the bishops (Catholics) or tradition (Orthodoxy) and the
bishops or the tradition function as the official interpreter
of the Bible. The primary Protestant default position on
the other hand identifies revelation with the actual words
of the biblical text. The amount of energy spent on apologetics to defend this view is far greater than the almost
non-existent "return on investment." Nevertheless, it is

the popular opinion here in America and everywhere American Protestants have taken their message. The Bible is viewed by some as a magical book with powers of its own in fundamentalism and thankfully this superstition is what the Gospel of Jesus Christ eliminates. One simply needs to turn to the great Christological hymns of the New Testament, particularly that of John 1:1–18 and Heb 1:1–4 where in both cases the revelation of God in the human figure Jesus of Nazareth trumps all revelation and becomes the sole hermeneutic lens by which to interpret all formerly conceived of revelation, even texts!

The Bible as a collection of sacred Jewish writings is not revelation but it does tell the human story from a specific perspective, through a certain people, and in that story there is an ongoing engagement with divinity. Thus we might say that there is revelation in the Bible. But we still have not brought our question to bear here: what is the relation between texts about the violent God found in Scripture and the nonviolent Abba of Jesus? Is it possible that it is not so much the relation of the Testaments that we need concern ourselves with but the question about violence the Bible raises? Is it possible that this ubiquitous theme, not only in Scripture but also in history and our daily news, is the key element we need to attend to discern revelation, the revelation of God? Is it possible that within the Bible, there are texts that reflect this growing awareness and disjunction between violence and shalom and that a seek solution for it?

If there is a focal point to the biblical canon, as a canon, it is certainly the death of Jesus. Paul will only know a crucified messiah and all the implications of that; the Gospels are but "passion narratives with extended introductions" and this is not to mention Hebrews or the slain lamb of the Apocalypse. Yes, it is death and violence or violent death that forms the heart of hearts of the Bible as canon. The death of Jesus is the can of worms in Christian theology. We can barely face it and what it means. We sacralize it in iconography and crosses we hang from our car mirrors or we turn it into the sacrificial act of a father slaying his own son with divine wrath. We make a transaction out of it and we completely fail to see that this story completely compromises our religiosity. It is a scandal of immense proportion and it is the greatest scandal to Christianity above all others.

In order to regain this apostolic perspective we, like they, must undergo the scandal of the cross. You may wonder of what the scandal of the cross consists; it consists of conversion. To see what is occurring on Calvary is a total shift of perspective and this is what the Bible as a collection of literature is seeking to do, to convert the way we see, think, and understand. It is to undergo a paradigm shift. When I teach this, I show a slide of Morpheus offering Neo the choice between the red pill and the blue pill in the film *The Matrix*. The blue pill will allow Neo to continue living in what he thinks is the real world. However, should Neo take the red pill, he will slip down the rabbit hole deeper than he could imagine. It does not matter how long you have been a Christian or not; it does not matter how deeply you have studied atonement theory. None of that can prepare one for the scandal of the cross and the conversion, or the paradigm shift it produces.

I invite you to examine the Passion Narrative of Mark (and that of John if you choose) and to ask the question: Where do you see God? The fact is that God is nowhere to be found in the Passion Narrative. Yet is this not the event in which Christians confess God was indeed present? If we read this narrative as it stands, and we do not see God present, we may need to reconsider just how it is God acts. The reading I asked you to do is in line with Martin Luther's "theology of the cross." In his 1518 Heidelberg Disputation theses, Martin Luther distinguished between a "theology of glory" and a "theology of the cross." Here are the pertinent theses:

19. That person does not deserve to be called a theologian who looks upon the "invisible" things of God as though they were clearly "perceptible in those things which have actually happened" (Rom 1:20; cf. 1 Cor 1:21–25).

20. He deserves to be called a theologian, however, who comprehends the visible and manifest things of God seen through suffering and the cross.

21. A theology of glory calls evil good and good evil. A theology of the cross calls the thing what it actually is.

22. That wisdom which sees the invisible things of God in works as perceived by man is completely puffed up, blinded, and hardened.

What Luther is saying is this: if you believe that God is revealed in historical processes (the ascension of the Führer for the German Nazis or the "anointing of a presidential candidate" for Americans), natural disasters or plagues, or in wealth, fame or power (or "signs and wonders"), then you are not seeing God but an idol of your own making. You have bought into a Deuteronomic hermeneutic (God blesses the good and curses the bad), and you also have a sacrificial way of thinking that justifies violence and exclusion in one form or another. This is a theology that requires a *deus ex machina*, a God who intervenes in human history on behalf of "God's own" (of course, always conceived of as "my group"). This is the predominant theology of American Protestant Christianity and its infected counterparts around the globe.

For Luther (and for me as well), God is not to be found in those things we "see" or would claim as "manifestations of God." If the Christian claim is that the most significant redemptive event is the crucifixion of Jesus, and in that event we cannot perceive God, and can in fact only confess that God is present in the most abyssal suffering, this overturns virtually all Protestant theology, especially the charismatic expressions which looks to signs of success or the supernatural as ways of claiming the presence of God. In short, God is not found where so many claim and God is to be found in "places" so many cannot see.

This is a perspectival shift. Try this little exercise—it is known as a Gestalt reading. Have a journal ready. Go back to the crucifixion scene and imagine yourself in the various "lives" of those around the cross: the soldiers, the interlocutors, the women. Write down what you think they could/would be thinking or feeling. Please do not read further until you have done this.

Do any of your figures see God present? How could they? Even if you hang around the Upper Room on Saturday, what is it you hear there? Try this exercise in imagination. What has happened to the theology of the disciples after Friday's events? What were they expecting of God? What were their disappointments? Fears?

Good Friday brings about a radical shift in perspective for it requires that everything we (and the disciples) thought we knew about God comes crashing to the ground. At Calvary all god concepts die. Luther looked at the wealth and power of the medieval Catholic Church, which because of that wealth and power could claim that God had "blessed" them and rejected the view of God which undergirded that claim. I look at American Protestant Christianity with its "prosperity gospel," its "self-help" gospel, its "signs and wonders" gospel and assert the same thing. It is Calvary that decimates these false doctrines of God. Calvary evacuates the legitimacy of any Superhero god, *deus ex machina* god, powerful god or god of might and glory. Instead, Calvary redefines God in the most radical way. The death of Jesus takes us beyond all of our theological illusions to the "suffering God" to the "powerless God." The twentieth-century theologian Jürgen Moltmann has made the best case for this in his second book, *The Crucified God*.

Now here is the second part of this exercise. The Apostle Paul contends that "God was in Christ reconciling the world to God's self" (2 Cor 5:16–20). Paul looked at Calvary through the same lens you have just looked. What was it that allowed him to see in the death of Jesus the supreme act of God (after creation)? What does it take to see God at Calvary?

It takes new eyes. Think back to Paul's experience on the Damascus Road. What was the question asked of him in his "vision"? Was it not related to Paul as an exponent of sacred violence, as one who would "do the right thing" and seek to purify the community by bringing death to others? Was not Paul being faithful to Torah? Surely he was, for Torah valorized the cleansing of the people. Phineas (Numbers 25) was held in high esteem for his act of murder which, according to Torah earned him a perpetual priesthood and an everlasting covenant. Paul is confronted on the Damascus Road with his prosecutorial theology. That which he perceived of as the solution was actually the problem.

What does this teach us? Going back to our Gestalt reading a moment ago, no one at Calvary thought that what they were doing was unjust. Yet it is this very injustice that becomes the focal point of Paul's conversion experience. In other words, revelation is first of all about us; it is anthropological before it is theological.

We cannot change our perception of God until we change our perception of ourselves in relation to God in Christ at Calvary. As long as we stand at the foot of the cross and seek to justify what is occurring there, we will never see God there. This is the problem of a sacrificial reading of the cross (or what is commonly known as penal substitution), for here the cross is justified by God; this simply places God on the side of the persecutors who also claim Jesus deserved what he got. As long as one shred of an attempt to justify the crucifixion of Jesus remains in our theology, we will always leave a door open for the sacrificial reading. Once this door is closed everything changes and we create "space" for the Holy Spirit to banish the scales from our eyes. It is only when we confess that God did not desire the death of His beloved Son that we can acknowledge that it was we alone (humanity) that needed that death. By so doing we can also for the first time begin to see just how we have played out these prosecutorial tendencies as Christians in relation to others, creating all manner of doctrines (from arbitrary election to penal atonement to afterlife punishment, not to mention our ethics) that we can use to justify marginalizing or ostracizing others. In other words, it is terribly wrong but possible to have a "holy" community if we have a "holy" god who justifies and grounds our acts of violence against others.

One of my goals has been to rethink Protestant (Evangelical) doctrine through this lens, leaving no stone (doctrine) unturned; if I were a younger man I might begin writing a systematic theology from this perspective. In the meantime I will use all of my intellectual and spiritual strength to topple this Protestant "theology of glory." There is a dividing line tearing Christianity apart today and it is the same exact line that Paul (and the writer of the Fourth Gospel and Luke-Acts [and Mark and to some extent Hebrews]) drew in the theological sand 2,000 years ago. Our task is not to make friends with this faux theology of Christian glory; our task is to speak truth to power and deconstruct it and show the masses why this pseudo-gospel is not Gospel. There can be no compromise here. To compromise on this point is to relegate Christianity to just another form of archaic religion grounded in sacred violence.

And this, God came to expose and crush and deliver humanity from in Jesus of Nazareth.

DISCUSSION QUESTIONS:

1. What are some of the ways people relate the two Testaments?

2. How significant is the role of violence in your day-to-day world?

3. How significant is the problem of violence in the Bible?

4. Why might an authentic Christian theology begin with Calvary, particularly in the twenty-first century?

2

MIMETIC THEORY

IN THIS CHAPTER WE will fulfill our first requirement; namely, we will learn a new anthropology, because definitions of what it means to be human are varied, often antiquated, or are a mish-mash of various systems of thought and superstition. I am not claiming that the theory of anthropology to which you are being introduced does not have its critics or challenges. As a grand theory, mimetic theory is comparable to Einstein's theory of relativity theory or Darwin's evolutionary theory in that it explains more of the data than previous theories. It also has its lacunae.

In this chapter I wish to cover three things: first, to tell you about René Girard, the designer of mimetic theory; second, to lay out a map of the theory and demonstrate how simple and elegant it is; and third, to address how the mimetic theory is being appropriated by members of The Colloquium on Violence and Religion in theological and biblical studies. Having laid this foundation we will then examine certain key Protestant doctrines in the subsequent chapters.

René Girard passed away in November 2015; his funeral service was a beautiful Requiem Mass. He was born in Avignon France on Christmas Day 1923, attended university in Paris during the German occupation of World War II, came to America in the late 1940s and began teaching French at an all-female college. Sometimes the French have a reputation for snobbery, but in this instance I don't think such is the case. René did not like the trashy French novels being used to teach the girls French and insisted that they study classic French novelists like Proust and Stendahl. That single change in literature may one day be the "official" starting point of the most significant paradigm shift in the human sciences. Girard discovered that characters in great or classic novels tended to behave similarly and began mapping out those behaviors concluding that the element of desire played a significant role in character relations and plot lines. In 1961, Girard produced his first book, *Deceit, Desire, and the Novel*, a study of the phenomenon of desire in several modern novelists, notably Stendahl, Proust, Cervantes and Dostoyevsky.

He and his family moved first to the Philadelphia area, where at Johns Hopkins, Girard produced his epoch making *Violence and the Sacred*. His research led him into all manner of literature in anthropological studies with particular attention to theorists of religion and the various theories of sacrifice in play. In this book Girard developed the first theory of religion that did not presuppose transcendence (or divinity) and instead explained where the concept first arose in the human species. More important, Girard argued that the juxtaposition of violence and transcendence lies at the heart of sacrifice. Sacrifice is the human solution to the problem of internecine violence. Girard is able to account for the rise of religion, and in her wake, human culture, in the practice of human sacrifice.

However it was his 1978 book, *Things Hidden Since the Foundation of the World,* that would rock the academic world, particularly that of biblical and theological scholarship. *Things Hidden* caused shock waves in that it brought the Bible into conversation with anthropology asserting that the biblical canon is part of human culture's discovery process. Secularists scoffed, theologians gasped, and the general public became quite interested in this new theory, in France at least. In 1982, two years after he came to Stanford University, Girard published the final element of the mimetic theory, *The Scapegoat.* Everything else in Girard's work supports the hypothesis generated in those four volumes. His work on ancient myths and legends, anthropology, literary studies, philosophy, psychology and his venture into theology and biblical studies is all supportive evidence for the mimetic theory as it develops in the 1960s and 1970s. Two biographies are currently being written on Girard by Cynthia Haven in the United States and Benoit Chantre in France.

René was not unlike a Renaissance philosopher in that he read quite broadly and engaged quite deeply in many disciplines. He was an inter-disciplinary researcher decades before it became semi-popular. His broad reading is what helped him to see that that the mimetic theory had a basis in reality, in our real human work-a-day world, and furthermore, that many modern sciences of humanity were making false assumptions and coming to fruitless, if not nihilistic, conclusions. Interestingly, as we will see shortly, the empirical science of mimetic theory is packed with confirmation of Girard's insights into the human condition, religion, and culture.

For our purposes it is important to note that René formulated the mimetic theory with the Bible as a conversation partner. This was the case even during the eleven years of research that culminated in the "first atheistic theory of religion," *Violence and the Sacred*. The Bible has always played an important role in mimetic theory and while the theory is itself a scientific theory in the strictest sense of the word, because it brings the Bible into conversations with human science, it also contains a theory of revelation. Some have seen this as a theatrical trick of Girard's to smuggle Christian apologetics into the laboratory of human life. Such is not the case. In Chapter 4, I will summarize a theory of the authority of Scripture apart from any theory of inspiration or canonization. The point is that the Bible is a key collection of texts for discerning the human condition, unlike any other texts before them. This difference will allow us to formulate a theory of revelation that is also a hermeneutic, much as Karl Barth did with the doctrine of the Trinity in *Church Dogmatics I/1*, but we will develop this insight "from below." If done properly, we will find congruence between the results of a mimetic reading of the Bible and the great Christian dogmas like the trinity, etc.

René continued to contribute to his work on mimetic theory with books on Shakespeare, Job, and von Clausewitz, as well as one on evil and satan and another on art. Several important interviews were also published during his "retirement years" (René stayed quite active until he was eighty-five!). My task is to summarize his work in three pages.

The mechanism of the mimetic theory, the actual "how it works," has been corroborated by the human and physical sciences and is easy to explain. Working out the implications of that for a theory of religion and culture might seem more difficult but again here archeological evidence establishes the theory as fact. At each turn as I explain the mimetic theory I will point to the science that has been done to verify the various aspects of the theory.

Remember the five questions I asked you in the previous chapter? If you were able to respond in the affirmative to at least one of the questions then learning the components of the mimetic theory, as a scientific theory of religion, will come effortlessly.

Mimetic theory has four distinct elements:

1. Mediated Desire

2. Rivalrous Escalation

3. Undifferentitation

4. Ritual Sacrifice

Have you ever wondered why, when you place two children in a room full of toys, they always end up fighting over the same toy? It has to do with mediated desire. All toys have equal value until one gets the interest of the first child. The second child non-consciously imitates that desire. Two children, one toy. We see this in story lines from antiquity to Hollywood and Bollywood. Two people sweet on the same person. The infamous French love triangle. Two persons vying for power. It is all around us if we look. The object of desire can be physical as in gold, wealth, or another person, and it can be non-corporeal as in power, fame, or recognition. If we examine our relationships we can see that most of our arguments and fights come because of mediated desire.

These are the relationships where slight disagreements turn into arguments and then in full blown fights and in some cases end in injury or death. Worse yet, we often end up wondering how in the world such an event escalated so quickly. Things are even worse in climates that are already polarized. What do law enforcement agencies worry about most after a terrorist attack or a mass shooting? They fear copycats or those persons who have interiorized vengeance modeling themselves after previous provocateurs. Mediated desire is competitive in nature and always leads to escalating rivalry in relationships. It also means that each new violent copycat will seek to one up their model. This is true at every level, "lone gunman," terrorist cells, or groups, and nation-states.

The engine that drives the human, as well as animal species is mimesis. Like our ancestors the great apes, mimesis leads to rivalry. In the primate population, according to Girard, mimetic rivalry is held in check by a dominance-submission behavior. The fighting ceases when one party submits to the other.[1] Aware of the debates between ethnologists and ethologists, Girard observes that mimetic patterns govern both human and animal species.[2] Mimetic behavior is not just a philosophical construct created out of whole cloth. In the past two decades, scientific research in a number of fields has shown that mimesis is hard wired in human biology and development.[3] We humans cannot but be mimetic.

---

1. Girard, *Things Hidden*, 90.

2. Girard, *Evolution and Conversion*, 101–3.

3. Garrells, *Mimesis and Science.*

Girard's contribution to the study of desire is to show that desire is mimetic. Humans non-consciously imitate the desire of the other. It is this nonconscious aspect of mimetic desire that blinds us to its reality. Jean-Michel Oughourlian observes "there is no innocent, harmless mimesis, and one cannot ritually imitate the crisis of doubles without running the risk of inciting real violence."[4] Mimetic behavior will always lead to rivalry or what Girard calls the process of doubling, where rivals become more and more like the other in the back and forth of the model-obstacle relationship. Rivalry between two individuals is not the happenstance chance of two independent desires for a single object; rivalry has its origin in mediated desire.[5] Thus it is that the abyss of "transcendence" between the model and the subject also becomes the place of death, for metaphysical desire cannot be fulfilled. In the human species, rivalry between model and subject will eventuate in violence. The juxtaposition of the need for self-transcendence and mimetic rivalry creates the space for the juxtaposition of violence and the sacred. As Girard notes, "violence and the sacred are inseparable."[6] In other words, humans create the concept of god out of having to deal with the problem of violence and self-transcendence. The problem of violence is *the* human problem and it is also *the* problem of religion.

Girard calls the notion of the autonomous individual the "romantic lie" fostered by the Enlightenment but which also has roots in Greek philosophy. We are not individual but to use the only neologism Girard coined, we are "*interdividual*." Several disciplines have verified

4. Girard, *Things Hidden*, 21.

5. Girard, *Violence and the Sacred*, 145.

6. Ibid., 19.

this empirically, from neuropsychology to child development, and it is supported by mimetic readings of authors like Flannery O'Connor and James Joyce. Mimetic theory participates in a much larger intellectual project, namely the turn to relationality in the twentieth century. LeRon Shults has demonstrated that in philosophy, literary studies, psychology, and philosophy, not to mention physics, there has been a turn away from perceiving "things in themselves" to understanding "things in relation."[7] This same shift can be seen in trinitarian discussions of the twentieth century as well, from Karl Barth to John Zizioulas and Catherine LaCugna, where God is perceived as "being-in-relation" rather than as the Platonic "to on" or being-in-itself. Perceiving human beings as interdependent is thus not novel but part of the larger scientific shift of this past century.

In terms of evolutionary biology we can recognize that the transition from ape to human did not go smoothly. As our brains became larger and thus the capacity for mimesis also grew, so did rivalry. Somewhere along the way in human development, the object of desire dropped out of the picture. Unlike our primate ancestors, we humans do not stop fighting once one person stops fighting. We continue fighting and in this continuance what was originally desired is no longer in focus. The focus has shifted to the fight and the only thing that matters, that will ensure survival, is winning that fight. Early humans would have wiped themselves out but for one thing and one thing only: sacrifice.

Sacrifice is ubiquitous in religion but oddly enough it is frequently assigned to "primitive worldviews" or some other pejorative and this is because the modern intellect

7. Shults, *Reforming* and *Postfoundationalist Task*.

thinks itself above all of the silliness surrounding offering animal sacrifices to deity, never once considering that the same sacrificial process continues to take place, and it is human sacrifice at that, under a more socially appealing secular form, namely the economy of the State. Jon Pahl has persuasively made the case that contemporary America is a huge temple machine replete with victims from youth to seniors, and people of color to women. [8]Only when we begin to see that we moderns have not, in fact, escaped the clutches of the ancient gods but that they have disguised themselves, will we recognize just how embedded we are in The Religious-Cultural Matrix.

Girard makes a clear and straightforward case that in the act of ritual (religious) sacrifice we find the juxtaposition of violence, the death of the victim, and divinity. Here's the thing: if we always come to sacrifice presupposing its origin in divine command, we will only ever be able to see sacrifice as necessary and justified by God. However, if like Jeremiah (7:20–23), we are willing to say that God did not write Leviticus (and the NIV is completely deceptive at this point with the addition of the word "just"), then we might inquire as to whence sacrifice originated and what how it functioned and here Girard observed that the principle of sacrifice *do ut des* ("I give in order to receive"), was an economy of exchange that could be found virtually everywhere. As modernity advanced and humanity became less and less dependent on "the gods," the principle of sacrifice was deemed primitive and unworthy of study for it all amounted to (in the eyes of the "enlightened") superstition. What Girard was able to do was to show that sacrifice had a very distinct social function: to slow if not stop inter-communal violence

8 Pahl, *Empire of Sacrifice.*

from escalating out of control. That is, sacrifice, first as a non-conscious activity, then as an intentionally ritualized activity, had as its purpose to use violence to stop violence like a homeopathic cure or a vaccine. Its effects were temporary and so had to be repeated and thus becomes the foundation upon which all human religion, and eventually culture, will be built.

The mimetic theorist first recognizes that humans are *interdividual* and thus mimetic and become entangled in model-obstacle relationships. These relationships escalate conflict and that conflict infects the community and exacerbates other mimetic conflicts in the community. It is a short step to the community reaching a crisis point where negative mimesis spirals out of control and the community is on the verge of self-annihilation. This is where sacrifice intervenes to be our savior. All it takes is for one person in the group to be blamed for the collective woes of the group and the group would turn on and "kill" (and for most of our human history, would eat) the human victim. They transferred their hostility toward each other onto the victim, who is a scapegoat, the one to blame for almost destroying the group.

But miracle of miracles! After the community has taken out their collective angst in the murder of the innocent, they experience a cohesion, for they have "cooperated" together, all against one. It is here we see the roots of the relationship between human competition (negative mimesis) and social cooperation that can only be achieved by the death of someone. Our entire way of being human, in other words, consists of destruction. We know no other way than that of deception and murder. Ancient myth, Sacred Scripture, great novelists, and the modern news all share this insight in common.

We will see in the next chapter the contribution that the Bible makes to this realization of the ubiquity of violence amongst humans, but for now it is only important to see that mimetic theory is not something new; we humans have known about it for several thousand years. From the musings of the pre-Socratic Heraclitus to those twentieth-century philosophers Arendt, Ricoeur, Foucault, and others, the entire tradition of western philosophy has been engaged, at one level or another, with the concerns of mimetic theory. The same is true in psychology, from Freud's Oedipal complex to systems theory to neurophysiology and genetics. Since, as Girard has noted, great novelists and thinkers also evidence elements of the mimetic theory, it is also the case that the same can be said of art and film in the twentieth century. The problem of violence is noted everywhere but few see why it is a problem. Like fish in water, most people are aware of violence as a social problem but because they are embedded in it, they cannot see it in their own lives, unless they, of course, are victims of that violence.

As an anthropological theory, and a recent one at that, mimetic theory has had its growing pains. So far it has stood up to every challenge and this is especially the case now when scientific research validates so many of Girard's central theses. For example, Girard postulated that religion predates human culture. That is humans were religious and it was religion that generated human culture (or what we would call "civilized" human culture). The archeological discoveries at Göbekli Tepe in modern Turkey have now validated this hypothesis of Girard's for there is a sacred site used for religious ritual several thousand years before the first known "civilizations."

Prior to Girard's rendering of the mimetic hypothesis on the origin of transcendence, there were two different ways to approach the study of religion. One could presuppose divinity and seek points of contact or analogies, particularly in the study of symbols (textual or ritual) or one could ask how it is that religion functions in a society, totally apart from the question of the existence of God. The former is known as the essentialist approach to religion; the latter is known as the functionalist. By recognizing elements of both in the mimetic theory, Girard is able not only to account for the similarities between the Christian faith and other myths and religions of antiquity, but also to articulate clearly its distinctiveness from other religions.

God is not a given in a mimetic rendering of sacred texts. Mimetic theory offers an explanation for how human beings came to "invent" their gods. A few generations ago it sufficed to say that humans named that which they could not tame or the unknown as the gods (like forces of the weather or the ocean). From a mimetic perspective that kind of thinking is quaint. In reality the origin of the gods is far darker. The gods are birthed in blood, human blood.

In *Violence and the Sacred,* Girard argues that ritual sacrifice provided the generative matrix out of which human religion, and also culture, would be born. The community that slaughters a human scapegoat engages in a double transference. They must first demonize or blame the victim for the woes that have befallen the community. For hundreds of thousands of years, this was perhaps totally non-conscious and sporadic, but eventually certain proto-humans would "recall" that the last time the community was in an upheaval, accusing someone solved the problem. Thus, one extended finger pointed in blame is imitated community wide and an innocent person (at least as innocent as anyone else) is demonized and the collective mimetic hostilities of the group are taken out on this poor soul. The cathartic act of displacing the community hostility onto the victim does not leave a void; it brings benefits, namely peace, unity, and cooperation. The earliest communities attributed these benefits to the victim. This constitutes the second transference. The victim, first demonized, is now divinized, and thus the gods are born. Violence and the sacred are the same thing!

From the repetition of this activity two other important elements also originate. The first is law or taboo. The community begins to recognize that certain "objects" provoke mimetic rivalry so they are placed off limits. Prohibitions thus seek to hedge mimetic desire. The second element is myth. Myths are the way the human community begins to articulate their experience of this self/community transcendence and they always tell the story of the community and its relation to the victim from the perspective of the community. The community, in myth, is always justified for the killing or expulsion of the victim, they are never portrayed as being wrong. How could they be wrong when they are 100 percent in agreement on this, and sometimes they even record that the victims agree with this assessment. Oedipus is an excellent example of this. Rituals, prohibitions, and myths are thus the three legs upon which human religion and culture build their empires.

This is an exceedingly brief and incomplete survey of the mimetic theory. There are plenty of excellent introductions listed in the bibliography. However, René Girard is not alone in developing the mimetic theory. Its intellectual foundations, scientific validation and implications for research as a heuristic tool have been validated time and again this past thirty years by researchers from The Colloquium on Violence and Religion (COV&R). This group formed in March 1990 at Stanford, California (I joined at the November 1990 meeting) to study mimetic theory. The first several years the study of mimetic theory in relation to Christianity and Judaism were center stage as we discussed the work of Raymund Schwager, Bruce Chilton, and Robert Hamerton-Kelly; then COV&R entered a phase where literary and cultural concerns became the focus and in the early 2000s it broadened out into all manner of sciences.

Back when I began studying mimetic theory in 1988 it was possible to read everything available in English by Girard or about mimetic theory in six months. That is no longer the case as research using the mimetic theory has exploded and the sheer amount of data produced by those who use the mimetic theory as an interpretive tool has expanded beyond the reach of a single interpreter. James G. Williams's *The Girardians* provides an adequate but by no means unbiased or complete account of the first twenty years of COV&R.[9]

Raymund Schwager, a pioneer of appropriating mimetic theory for theological and biblical work, published *Must There Be Scapegoats?* in 1978. Girard had published *Things Hidden* that same year and the recently published correspondence between Schwager and Girard highlights mutual influence on their respective books. Both used the groundbreaking work on sacrifice and religion in *Violence and the Sacred*. While it was Girard's book that would be the academic breath of fresh air, as it advanced

9. Williams, *The Girardians*.

a non-sacrificial reading of the Bible, Schwager's work on the problem of violence in the Bible, especially those texts where God was violent, is a necessary complement to *Things Hidden*. Schwager, a Jesuit trained as a theologian, was able to integrate the historical-critical method and biblical exegesis with the mimetic theory and develop a model of the science of theology with cues taken from Hans Urs von Balthasar's *Theodrama*. Schwager's students at the University of Innsbruck continue to develop his "dramatic" approach in a series of monographs. Schwager's work has not gained the same notoriety as Girard's work, but as one who has known both personally and has been at this business of mimetic theory for almost thirty years, I would argue that any approach to Scripture that does not take into account Schwager's trail-blazing work is doomed to re-invent the wheel.

Though the early years of COV&R studies related to Christianity and the Gospel, focusing on the problem of God requiring sacrifice or of God expressing retribution and how these texts can be read in a totally new light, as the 1990s progressed, the focusing issue became atonement. Over the course of the next decade a number of dissertations and important books would be written on atonement. Anthony Bartlett published *Cross Purposes,* which examined in fine detail the underlying sacrificial elements in Anselmian atonement theory; J. Denny Weaver used Schwager's and my work on Hebrews in his *The Nonviolent Atonement*; and S. Mark Heim produced the first full-scale reading of atonement and sacrifice in the Bible in the light of mimetic theory in *Saved from Sacrifice*. I made my own contributions in essays and in my book *The Jesus Driven Life,* where I explored mimetic theory as a hermeneutic. Interestingly enough, in the mid-1980s

Gerhard Forde appropriated only *Violence and the Sacred* in his essay on atonement in the Lutheran *Christian Dogmatics* but this work is sadly too little known. In the chapters that follow I will make reference to these and other works of the members of COV&R who continue to make contributions to a mimetic reading of the Bible.

The implications of using the mimetic theory as an interpretive tool for reading the Jewish and Christian canons are staggering, far reaching, and life changing. They are staggering because mimetic theory is not rocket science; it is easily grasped and when it is grasped it leads to a paradigm shift. The implications are far reaching because for they impact every single Christian doctrine by simply changing the way the human is understood. Mimetic theory is life changing inasmuch as the spirituality and the ethics of what Rebecca Adams calls "positive mimesis" is oriented to love, compassion, mercy and forgiveness. As I said in the first chapter, for many, learning mimetic theory was akin to Neo taking the red pill in *The Matrix*. Rather than presupposing a god, by applying a mimetic reading to the Bible we become aware just how much we Christians have made God in our own image and after our own likeness. It is only in first seeing this that we can then speak of revelation. Revelation is first of all about us and our false gods; then it is about the apocalyptic invasion of God to deliver us from the Matrix of Religious Violence. This is the journey of the next chapter.

DISCUSSION QUESTIONS:

1. Have you encountered the mimetic theory before? If so where and did it have an impact on you?

2. How would you describe the four parts of the mimetic theory to someone who had not heard it?

3. How large of a theme is "sacrifice" in the Bible? In the Gospels?

4. What are some of the implications for developing a mimetic anthropology in relation to Christian theology?

3

RELIGION AND REVELATION

WHY DO YOU PICK up a Bible? Why are you going to read it? How do you read it? Martin Luther said that "Scripture has a wax nose." The Reformation did not create *de novo* the problem of multiple interpretations of Scripture; throughout church history there have always been competing interpretations of Scripture and different hermeneutical approaches. One could mention the schools of Antioch and Alexandria in the early church or the vibrant plethora of methods within Catholicism in the fifteenth century. This is not to say that the Reformation did not bring new approaches to the Bible; rather, it is simply to note that the question of hermeneutical method has always been a matter of conversation and contention in Christianity.

A further rift was brought about by reading the Bible through "enlightened" eyes and the development of the historical-critical method. Beginning in the late seventeenth century, the Bible began to be perused not as a source of divine revelation but as a book like any other book, and the methods one applied to all other literature to discern meaning and significance were applied to the Bible. The reaction of Protestantism was to sacralize the Bible and to create a theory of the inspiration of the Bible that was in itself an implicit hermeneutic. The Protestant claim was that the Spirit located in the text ("in-spired") was also in the believer. Combined with the radical winds blowing through the seventeenth and eighteenth centuries in the political concepts of democratic government, Rosseau's social contract, and the rise of "the autonomous individual," this heady mix of the Bible, the Spirit, and the believer meant that not only could any person read the Bible, but that any person could interpret the Bible. Furthermore, since each person had the same Spirit in themselves as was found in the Bible, each person could claim that their interpretation was the correct (divine) one. When Calvin wrote about the intimate correlation between Word and Spirit in the sixteenth century, I don't think he had in mind 4,000 different types of Baptists or 41,000+ Christian denominations and sects we see today.

One might think that 41,000 different interpretations would make theology a difficult task especially when you add to that all the variety of interpretations produced by the academy, especially in the past forty years with the rise of socially located theologies. Modern theological studies have given up on seeking a common thread and have given themselves over to the study of the religious language of these various communities. Entering her third millennium, Christianity is adrift at sea. It may claim a relationship to the Bible but that relationship will always be a flawed relationship, not because of the perfection or the imperfection of the text but because of the reader. Scripture does indeed apparently have a wax nose.

Karl Barth did the lion's share of the work clearing the ground in his iconic *Römerbrief* published in December 1918. Barth's entire legacy can be summed up in his phrase, "Let God be God!" His *Church Dogmatics*, *The Barmen Declaration* and up to his final lectures on *Evangelical Theology* this theme resounds over and over: God has revealed God's self in Jesus Christ. From Barth's perspective the Church had too many other starting points rather than the name Jesus Christ. Combined with the new interest in the life of Jesus following Albert Schweitzer's *The Quest of the Historical Jesus*, both theological and biblical studies (with its biblical theology and *Heilsgeschichte* schools) made the turn to a more christologically centered reading of the Bible.

There is a need for all Protestantism, confessional and non-confessional, liberal and conservative, orthodox and sectarian, to go through the school of Karl Barth. Barth's early critique of religion and of Christianity as a religion, in the light of the Gospel, is particularly necessary. Barth distinguished between religion and revelation. Christianity may be related to the Gospel but neither can be identified with one another for Christians have in many ways been poor witnesses. They failed to heed the apostolic witness to God's revelation instead substituting some other thing or idea as a starting point. The default position of Evangelicalism and Fundamentalism, including the Pentecostal and Charismatic tradition, is to begin theology with a theory of the inspiration and authority of Scripture. Barth was able to take the Reformed and Evangelical tradition and shift its ground away from the

Bible and to Jesus Christ. (However, as a good Reformed churchman, Barth had to include the authority of the pulpit, and thus of the Bible, in his theory of revelation.)

In our time however, a more important historical fact has dominated theological concern: the Shoah. Deep and powerful questions of theodicy and human suffering shine as the Pharos lighthouse in theological studies from 1950 on. The work of Simone Weil, Dietrich Bonhoeffer, Jürgen Moltmann, Dorothee Sölle, Paul van Buren, Dietrich Ritschl, and of course all of the theologies of social location amply testify to this. Contemporary Christian theology is suffused with the question of human suffering and God's relation to it. All of this has come about due to the turn in Jewish-Christian relations following the Holocaust. Jewish and Christian scholars began working together, learning to see one another through each other's eyes. Christians began to learn to see through the eyes of the victim. At the beginning of the twenty-first century we have seen all manner of racism and violence against those deemed "the other," any number of regional conflicts and wars, migrations of millions of refugees in Europe, Africa, and Asia. Add to this the growing number of mass shootings, police killing unarmed civilians, civilians targeting and killing law enforcement, terrorist attacks, human trafficking, and slavery and you can make a case that violence is a significant social problem that humans have not yet figured out or resolved.

A Christian theology that does not acknowledge from the outset the problem of violence and ask about its character and function and origin is a theology without hands or feet. Jesus viewed the Jewish cultural collection of sacred writings Christians calls the Old Testament as bookended by murder. In Matthew 23, Jesus excoriates the religious authorities, with their vested interests in the religious-political establishment around the Temple in Jerusalem. He tells them they reject God's prophets and punish, torture, and execute them. He then cites story of the murder of Abel from Genesis 4 and that of Barachaiah from the "closing book" of the Jewish scriptures, 2 Chronicles 24. Jesus' culture, like our own, was saturated with the problem of retributive violence.

Recognizing the existential problem of violence is not difficult—all one has to do is turn on the news or read the newspaper. If it bleeds, it leads. Readers of the Bible have had a difficult time recognizing that the Scriptures also frame God's narrative as one of violence. God floods the world, destroys cities in firestorms, seeks to murder Moses, commands genocide, delights in the slaughter of innocents, even babies, brings plagues, and is often in a wee bit of a testy mood. The real problem does not lie in the fact that the Bible says all of this; no, the real problem is first the presumption that because it is said in the Bible it is true. *That* is the problem. The real problem is the underlying view of the Bible as a book divinely inspired, dropped from heaven, superintended authorship. Call it what you want, in this view, "God said it. I believe it. That settles it." Well, pardon me, but that doesn't settle anything. It simply says you have a hermeneutic method and your hermeneutic method or way of reading the Bible is not subject to criticism; for to criticize the method is to criticize the "God" who wrote the Bible.

If such is the case, woe to just about every redactor, editor, or copyist of the Bible. The Deuteronomist is just as guilty as the corrector of Sinaiticus. Woe to Jeremiah the prophet for saying God did not write the Levitical Code (Jeremiah 7). Woe to Jesus who selectively cites Scripture, adding and omitting phrases. Shame on the apostle Paul for doing the same kind of cherry-picking when it comes to the Jewish Scriptures. Or perhaps the woe is on the reader who assumes from the get-go that the Bible as a whole is all God's Word. Perhaps there is another way to read this collection of literature that notices a trajectory from the Torah through the Prophets and into certain streams of Second Temple Judaism. Perhaps Jesus, Paul, and other apostolic writers were onto something, something that they derived from their own sacred scriptures. What was this hermeneutic that Jesus and some of the apostolic community developed?

There are two sides by which we can denote this hermeneutic using the work of Jewish scholars Michael Fishbane and Sandor Goodhart. Fishbane shows that the Jewish scriptures contain an intentional editing process, a reworking of the tradition; the laws and the stories of the Bible are engaging in critical appraisal of previous forms of these laws and stories. In other words, the very ones passing on the tradition modified the tradition and engaged in what is known as "content-criticism," a far more substantive and radical project than mere text criticism. Goodhart has shown that there is a hermeneutic principle at work in this "content-criticism," which he identifies as "the law of anti-idolatry."

If Goodhart and Fishbane[1] are correct, then one can characterize "content-criticism" as part of the internal hermeneutic of the Bible. There is a need to "rightly divide the word of truth" (2 Tim 2:15) for it consists of that which needs to be divided, religion and revelation. The god of religion, the Janus-faced deity is exposed and the true God is revealed when this division occurs. What char-

1. Fishbane, *Biblical Interpretation*.

acterizes this God? "The anti-idolatrous God is the God of repentance or *teshuvah*, the God of turning back, the God who commands you to recognize the path you have been following in order that you may give it up." "To live anti-idolatrously is to live from the point of view of God, from the perspective of the Creator, from the Creative source of the universe."[2] The God of the Jewish scriptures who calls humanity to repentance, the gracious, merciful and compassionate God is *Ha-Shem*, the One with the Unpronounceable Name, Maker of all that exists.[3] This is the anti-idolatrous God. What then does the idolatrous god look like? Exactly as all sacrificial, arbitrary, vengeful, angry, retributive gods look; in short, the idolatrous God is the god of archaic religion. The idolatrous god needs victims. *Ha-Shem* comforts victims. This perspective has a specific angle related to the question above about the end of our human dramas.

With this we recognize immediately that there are at least two voices, two perspectives in the Scriptures. There *appears* to be the voice of *Ha-Shem*, the true God, a loving, compassionate deity; there also *appears* to be the voice of a god like all other gods. It is important to notice that this is not Marcion's error. The Jewish tradition juxtaposes an archaic view of God (religion) alongside revelation from the true God. Marcion taught that there were two gods and the lesser god was the Jewish god while the higher god was the Christian god. Not Goodhart, Fishbane, Girard, nor myself are saying any such thing. Marcion had asked the right question about the problem of the relation of violence and divinity, the same question

2. Goodhart, *Sacrificing Commentary,* 198–99.

3. In *Virtually Christian*, Anthony Bartlett uses the term "No-God" to capture the reality of transcendence that has nothing to do with human religion, idols and concepts of God.

Girard would ask nineteen hundred years later in *Violence and the Sacred*. Marcion's dualistic solution was rightly rejected by the church for it separated the Creator from the Redeemer. The internal critique of religion by revelation found in the Bible is the voice of God over against all human constructs of divinity, in other words, "the principle of anti-idolatry." The practice of content-criticism is a key element of the internal biblical hermeneutic, and one that Jesus and Paul deployed.[4]

At stake here is nothing less than revelation itself, for if revelation is confused with religion then the God we claim is the true God is just like all the other gods. Our claim that only our God is real while all the others are fakes and idols turns out to be no more than theological provincialism. What is actually at work in the Jewish and Christian scriptures, by contrast, is theological criticism.[5] Now I am aware that Karl Barth would eschew the practice of content-criticism (*Sachkritik*), particularly the way his colleague Rudolf Bultmann practiced it. Nevertheless the iconic anti-religious theme of Barth's reading of Romans and the shattering of Christian confidence in its theology is identical to the Hebrew prophetic content-criticism of Torah. The Hebrew prophets, Jesus, the apostles, Barth,

4. See *The Jesus Driven Life* for examples.

5. All theologies of Christendom, which claim that the creator of the world is the sponsor of human empire, are necessarily provincial. They cannot be otherwise because they must do two things simultaneously: justify structural violence in the name of God and claim that the gods of rival civilizations are either demonic or nonexistent. These historically dominant theological projects are a direct and thorough reversal of the anti-provincial trajectory of Hebrew prophets and Christian apostles and richly deserve every postcolonial and relativistic regime of euthanasia that has been administered to them under the name of "Comparative Religion" in the modern secular academy.

and Girard all clear the ground by distinguishing between religion and revelation.

The first question to ask is not "What is God like?" but "What can mimetic theory teach us about the gods humans have created?" For now not even the category of "God" can be a given, we cannot assume we either know or don't know "God." The only thing we can say for certain about the gods is that they require sacrifice. As we saw earlier, when Girard uncovered the implicit economy of exchange in sacrifice and correlated it with mimetic behavior, he was able to show how the double-transference took place with regard to the victim of the mob-community. The victim is the first figure both de-monized (blamed) and divinized (praised). There are two important consequences of this insight.

First, there are two sides to every story. However, if it wasn't for the Bible, we would not know that! Myths only contain one voice, for myths are written by the victors (i.e., by the persecuting community). Richard Golson's excellent study notes that Girard's definition of myth does not fit neatly into more conventional categories for while Girard "shares the view that myths are not precise accounts of historical occurrences, he does argue that they originate in real or historical events and are in fact distorted representations of these events."[6] Humans didn't just sit around one day and look at the sky and wonder where it came from and if there might be a higher power. The awareness or consciousness of transcendence came through the blade of a knife, or the end of a club, or the tip of a spear. Human consciousness was birthed in death, not an existential fear of death like Heidegger would have

6. Golson, *René Girard and Myth*, 61.

us believe, but in actual violent death. In the beginning was the weapon . . . and the mob.

Myths are the ways we humans tell the stories of those we have demonized, killed, then divinized, and all of the superstitious and magical powers we give these poor sods when we make them our gods. Myths are not history but they bear witness to history, to murder most foul. In myth the victim has no voice or their voice is made to agree with the voice of the community as in the Oedipus Rex cycle of myths and dramas. The clearest example of pure myth in the Bible is the story of Achan in Joshua 7. Girard identifies four characteristics of myth: "a generalized loss of differences (the first stereotype), crimes that 'eliminate differences' (the second stereotype), and whether the identified authors of these crimes possess the marks that suggest a victim, the paradoxical marks of the absence of difference (the third stereotype)."[7] Violence is the fourth stereotype. One can see the first in the failure of Israel's military campaign due to internecine squabbling as well as in the leveling effect of the lottery. The second comes as a prologue as to why God has turned God's back on Israel—someone has violated the taboo. The third element, the marks of a victim, are a bit more difficult to tease out, as well they should be if the mythologizers have done their due diligence. What singles Achan out, however, is that other than the Lord's voice and Joshua's voice, Achan is the only other voice in the story and he agrees completely with that of the persecuting community, represented by God and Joshua. If that is not apparent what immediately follows should seal the deal: the mob lynching of an entire family

7. Girard, *The Scapegoat*, 24.

system—death by stoning. This is the all-against-one of mythological victimage.

Like Achan, victims in myths either do not speak, their voices have been silenced, or what they say reflects the community's judgment. This is also true, for example, in the Oedipus myths and dramas. The truth as to the true murderer, hidden in Homer but revealed by Sophocles as the mob begins to reveal that maybe the one who did the deed is not really the one responsible. That much is there, at least in Sophocles. The Bible takes this further and we can see this particularly in Job who is the anti-Oedipal type in the Bible. Job refuses time and again to buy into the accusations of guilt hurled at him. He righteously speaks against his interlocutors, wrongly called "friends," and three times threatens to take God to court and file suit against the Almighty! Job's protests are the exact opposite of Oedipus or Achan. The dialogues of the book of Job is "an extended psalm," much like we find throughout the Psalter. Many are the psalms where the victim's voice is given (e.g., Psalm 22). The sheer number of laments of those downtrodden and marginalized found in the Jewish scriptures is what sets these texts apart from all other world mythologies. In the Jewish sacred texts, the victim finally has a voice.

The best example of this is the founding murder myth in Genesis 4 where Cain slays Abel. Murder myths can be found in many cultures and usually involve a set of twins or rivals family members. The founding murder myth of the city of Rome found in Titus Livius (Livy) is a good analogue to the Cain and Abel story. Both stories have a sacrificial element, both involve mimetic rivalry over an object of desire. Both escalate out of control and eventuate in death. In Livy, Remus is guilty for trespassing the boundary stones set up by Romulus. The same guilt can be found in the Oedipus cycle—as we have already noticed—and in the Enuma Elish (where Tiamat is the guilty divinity).

The founding murder myth of Cain and Abel is the first such myth to give voice to the victim. In this case, Abel's voice cries out from the ground for retribution. God hears that voice, but does not heed the cry for retributive justice; instead, God marks Cain to stop all future vengeance. This distinction between the [muted] voice of the victim in myth and the vocality of the oppressed within the pages of the Bible cannot be understated. In the next chapter, we will explore how these insights help to distinguish between voices in Scripture.[8]

The second important consequence of recognizing the effects of the double-transference onto the victim is the insight that language is bloody. Girard, examining the human process of scapegoating, argues that the victim of scapegoating is the originary matrix out of which language is born. The victim is the pre-historical symbol. First, the victim is blamed for the woes of the community, then ritually killed (and eaten), then divinized by that very same community that sought to account for the "blessings" of peace, concord, and cooperation. The victim is thus demon and god, bane and blessing (and this is the origin of the Janus-faced god). The victim is the first "thing" with a double meaning; the victim is what gives rise to our communication abilities as a species. The victim is the ground of our linguistic capacity and ability to symbolize and thus be able to coin phrases like "the apple of my eye." Humans are not simply linguistic creatures;

8. The next few paragraphs have been adapted from *What the Facebook? Volume 1*.

we are the species that symbolizes. As Paul Ricoeur would say, "language has a surplus of meaning."

Language is bloody. It is not clean. Language did not originate in some heaven of heavens but in the abyss of false accusation, death, and cannibalism. Language is full of lies and deception. Language masks. Language, therefore, is inadequate to bring divine communication. It took the real act of the death of Jesus and his pronouncement of forgiveness to overturn language. His bloody cross spoke truth to language in language. His resurrection vindicated his truthfulness to language by language.

Language is bloody; we ought not to trust it completely. This is how we got to this post-modern state we are in where many experience everything as relative. The hermeneutics of suspicion (Marx, Freud, Nietzsche, Feuerbach) grounds all modern discourse. Michel Foucault and Jürgen Habermas have shown how power agendas take our language and use it for their own gain. In George Orwell's *1984*, the author writes about our capacity for "doublespeak." In other words, our current condition of deconstructing human communication—recognizing its dark side and its power grabs—is essential if we are going to move past the pre-modern emphasis on the purity of language (represented by certain Jewish, Muslim, and Christian theories of the inspiration of sacred texts).

If you find yourself a post-modern Christian but still feel you have to hold onto pre-modern views of the Bible, know this: language is bloody, deceptive, and manipulative because human symbolic communication is corrupted by our scapegoating tendencies. Yet, just as God did in the dying Jesus, God is able to "speak" to us a redemptive word, a word that heals and brings peace. As Karl Barth puts it "revelation is a gain to language." God's self-revelation at the heart of the victimage mechanism is also redemptive; we call this at-one-ment. In the cross God has also brought truthfulness back to language. But language can only be true if it bears this cruciform character, if it speaks honestly about the "other," if it speaks forthrightly about its own persecutory character.

All of this is what one learns by viewing all reality through a singular lens: that of Jesus Christ crucified, the true Word of God. This of course is the well-known position of Paul (1 Corinthians 1). Martin Kähler is credited with saying that Mark is "a passion narrative with an extended introduction." The Gospels of Mark, Luke, and John share this cruciform emphasis in their structures and the Fourth Evangelist has extended it to her vocabulary (*Döppelganger* or words with double meaning like *doxazo* or *hypsao*). This is not to mention the sermon "to the Hebrews." It is not enough to say that the New Testament is Christologically focused; that is too general. For every great apostolic writer was not looking at Jesus the person but at what Jesus underwent in his death, resurrection, and ascension. The latter two were only given meaning by the former. When one begins here, Calvary functions as an episteme, a starting point and it will have implications for everything that is said after that about God, humanity, creation, and history. The cross of Christ leaves nothing untouched. It heralds the death of one age and the promise of another.

In the same way, Christian theology that takes into account the voice of the victim will notice that the Passion Narrative has the same identifying marks as myth. The Passion Narrative is structured as myth. One could call it Christian myth if not for the fact that this narrative subverts and overturns any conventional reading of myth and provides an historical account of a human person, Jesus of Nazareth, playing the same role as other unknown and nameless victims of ritual social scapegoating. This Jesus is innocent. It is the victim in the story of the cross who has a voice. Jesus does not agree with his persecutors that he is guilty. He remains silent as a lamb. As Girard says, the science of the Gospel is the way it interprets myth.

Like Barth, who argues for theology as a science, mimetic theory also proposes itself as a scientific theory. Unlike other anthropological sciences, however, mimetic theory recognizes a) that the theory is already contained within the Bible itself and b) that the "*theological* point of contact" with science is the victim (who is the ground of a new logic [*logos*]). The biblical revelation is not an abstract religious, pious, or devotional message but the concrete manifestation of God, in incarnate life, especially as the Crucified. It is the Passion Narrative that exposes the religious operation of mimetic scapegoating and thus decodes that upon which the effectiveness of such activity depends—namely, myth. Apart from the demythification process found in the Bible culminating in the Passion Narrative we would not even know what scapegoats were. The Bible provides the key to unmasking the foundational deception of myth along with its cultural and religious edifice, *including those texts in the Bible that share the mythological perspective. The Bible is in the process of deconstructing itself.*

> Actually it takes place earlier in these great stories in the Jewish Bible. In myth, the scapegoat is always guilty. But in the Joseph story, while Joseph is obviously the scapegoat of his brothers, the Bible doesn't tell us he's guilty, that he's bad like his brothers. It says it's the brothers who made up those stories. In other words,

these are not myths at all. These stories are the truth of myths. The scapegoat phenomenon only works when it is nonconscious. You never say, "I had a scapegoat." If you have a scapegoat, you deem him guilty. That's what myths say. But the biblical texts and the Gospels tell you the victim is only a scapegoat. He is not really guilty. Therefore, you have scientific proof that the Bible is revealing something, and especially the Gospels, because they become more and more explicit that the victim is innocent and Christ is the most innocent of all victims. If you're an anthropologist, you can see that myth and the Gospels have the same structure. You have a big crisis that ends with a scapegoat ritual, and the victim is turned into a god. This is true of myths, but this is true of the Gospels too. That's why anthropologists will tell you that myths and the Gospels are the same stories, the same religion. You have to understand what a scapegoat is to understand the difference. The Christians should have done that years ago, whereas they are scared of anthropologists who don't know what they are doing.[9]

The voice of the biblical victim, which is muted in myth, runs from Abel through Torah and the historical and prophetic books and especially in the wisdom literature of the Jewish scriptures all the way to Jesus of Nazareth and beyond him to the Christian martyrs of the Apocalypse of John. Human culture depends on its scapegoats in order not to implode. Caiaphas recognized this when he averred that it was better for one (innocent) man to die than a nation should perish. At Calvary that age-old all-against-one mechanism cranked itself up for the usual

9. Hardin, *Reading the Bible with René Girard*, 84.

bloodletting and was utterly sabotaged, forever unable to bear the load it had created by juxtaposing violence and the sacred. The death of Jesus shatters that because of the type of victim he become or as Hebrews says "Jesus' blood speaks a better word than that of Abel's."

The cross offers a different view on what is occurring in this purely human ritualized activity of scapegoating. It offers God's point of view. It offers forgiveness. The voice of Calvary is the voice of the forgiving victim. Unlike mythology, the victim of Calvary is seen in the splendor of his innocence; his voice is neither muted nor silenced. Unlike the innocent but retributive victim that we find unveiled in the Jewish scriptures, Jesus does not seek vengeance but actively proffers forgiveness. This is the voice of revelation and it too can be found in the Jewish scriptures but it develops over time and particularly in the literature produced in and around Israel's first exile.

Two perspectives mean two different ways of interpreting the same event. The first perspective has two voices: the victim of myth and the innocent but retributive victim. These have been and still are the voices of religion and the gods of religion. The voice of revelation—the voice of Shalom, the voice of G-d—is a voice that is non-coercive, non-violent. However, this *via negativa* does not describe the positive character of this divinity and words like love and grace, mercy and compassion hardly seem able to carry the load of the reality they signal. The voice of religion, embedded in sacrifice, evidenced in the central role played by an economy of exchange, can at best produce innocent but retributive victims, persons who need the scales balanced. The voice of revelation balances the scales once and for all by "placing all under disobedience" in order that "God might have mercy on all."

Religious reading of the text is only capable of a sacrificial interpretation. This reading can be devotional or it can be historical-critical; it can be allegorical or literal; it can be ancient, medieval or modern. Its forms are endless, it is always a question of perspective. Are we reading these sacred texts through the eyes of the forgiving victim, through the revelatory lens of that event which alone is able to deconstruct this Babel of Modern Culture and help usher in a Vibrant Shalom Community? Or are we reading these texts through the eyes of the crowd, the mob, the human community intent in every way on justifying why death is necessary and essential? Which lens are we using? No matter how many hermeneutical alternatives there are on the table, they can all be divided into two categories: those that are sacrificial and those that are non-sacrificial.

We have sought to come at this business of a cross-centered epistemology and hermeneutic from several angles. In the next chapter we will ask what these insights mean for understanding the character of the Bible (the [so-called] biblical meta-narrative) and for the authority of the biblical text. In so doing we can also begin to explore some of the implications of a mimetic anthropology for Christian doctrine. Some critics of Girard misrepresent him and claim he wants to do away with accepted or orthodox Christian dogma. Nothing could be further from the truth. Girard has contended (and I would concur) that mimetic theory clears up many of the problems created by metaphysics for Christian theology and is eminently orthodox.

DISCUSSION QUESTIONS:

1. How would you describe the state of the Christian religion in your area?

2. How would you describe the prophetic "critical principle" and why might it be crucial for understanding the Bible?

3. How are victims described in the news? Upon what might it depend?

4. The author contends that there is a dividing line between sacrificial and non-sacrificial interpretations of the Bible and that the former is not Gospel. Do you agree or disagree and why?

4

INTERLUDE: HOLY SCRIPTURE

RATHER THAN BEGIN WITH a theory or doctrine of the inspiration of the Bible, let us simply approach the Bible as human literature as we do any literature. By so doing we avoid all of the complications that go with trying to establish a theory of both revelation and inspiration prior to reading the Bible. At this point we are abandoning the correlation the Reformers made between Word and Spirit. This is no longer an option. Over 41,000 different types of Protestants and their chaotic plethora of inter-pretations have made a lie of that line of thinking. The allegedly divine text does not seem to be in the business of guaranteeing true theology.

When we bring the Bible into conversation with ancient literature, from perhaps as early as the first writ-ten texts of the Bible—800 BCE to the last written texts, say 120 CE— and read the Bible alongside literature from antiquity it is very clear what the Bible is doing. It is in the process of differentiating the True God, the God-With-No-Name, from the way we humans have always constructed the concept of divinity. In other words, how does a God who is purely Love and Light distinguish God's self from the human capacity to assume that deity *eo ipso* is Janus-faced? How could such a God reveal the authentic character of God's purely gracious and compassionate self in a system of religion that required economies of exchange? How could such a God, who is love and only shalom, demonstrate such love and shalom in a world guided and maintained in sacred violence?

The Jewish scriptures bear witness that whatever else it may have taken for God to reveal God's self, it took time. From the call of Abraham some 1,200 years before Jesus, the scriptures weave a narrative woven of God calling Israel and of Israel's stormy relationship with God. Through it all, like scarlet thread, is woven bits and pieces of the composers seeing something new in these sacred texts. It might be in the way laws about slaves differed from their contemporaries. It may have been about caring for the marginalized and defenseless, the widows and the orphans. It may have been the laments that accompanied Judaism through the exile and beyond. Israel's relationship with her God is the story of a great wrestling match (Gen 32:22–32). One could easily deploy the story of Jacob wrestling with the figure who represents the Most High as a metaphor for the function of the Jewish canon. These texts require wrestling. They are not a monolithic voice.

Girard says,

> In a way, the achievement of the Bible is all the greater once you realize that before the prophetic tradition there were the worst

fundamentalists that ever lived. The Bible is a
constant process of conversion, which is not a
single voice but which has great multiplicity of
voices. If it were a given in the Bible, if the Bible
were not a history of the human spirit instruct-
ed by the Holy Spirit, by God, if it were not that
kind of history as well as the telling of stories, if
we could not see that history in the writing of
the Bible, the Bible would be less valuable than
it is. Do you see what I mean? We cannot go
back to a view of the Bible that takes every word
as revealed and sacred, where you cannot touch
it or interpret it.[1]

The fact is that both perspectives, that of religion
and that of revelation, run through the Jewish and Christian canons. The dividing line is not between the canons,
but within them. Girard refers to the Jewish scriptures as
"texts in travail" but the same could be said of the Christian canon. Jude would be a good example of a sacrificial
Christian theology; Romans would be an example of a
non-sacrificial Christian theology. One could make a case
that Matthew's meta-narrative of Jesus is still embedded
in Second Temple Jewish eschatology and has both a
sacrificial and a non-sacrificial approach to Christology,
whereas Mark, Luke, and the Fourth Evangelist are non-
sacrificial in their respective Gospels. In short, what we
have is an act of God, the revelation of God's very character in the life of a human being, at the end of a patient
pedagogical process. This pedagogical view of history
is ancient and can be found in both the pagan and the
Christian world, particularly in Irenaeus and Clement of
Alexandria.

---

1. Hardin, *Reading the Bible with René Girard*, 58.

The Bible is a collection of sacred writings "between myth and Gospel." There are indeed texts that support the view of the persecuting community or figure and there are texts that tell the side of the victim. Both texts are co-mingled in every single document of the Jewish canon, which is why Girard refers to the Jewish Bible as a "text in travail." It advances and retreats in its developing insight about humanity, God and violence. Raymund Schwager has shown that in the Jewish Bible there is a definite trend separating God from violence as it develops over time.[2] These two perspectives—that of the mob and that of the victim—are the two hermeneutic alternatives. It is important to remember that the victim of religion has two types, that of the muted victim (world mythology) and that of the innocent but retributive victim. Both types of victim continue the cycle of violence; nothing is ever solved. Gospel is when the biblical texts clearly articulate the voice of the innocent victim who seeks not vengeance, which would continue the cycle of violence, but mercy and forgiveness, which alone can stop it. As the writer to the Hebrews says, "Jesus' blood speaks a better word than that of Abel." Here is a diagram.[3]

2. Schwager, *Must There Be Scapegoats?*

3. Thanks to Richard Beck for creating this diagram from a talk I gave.

The Voices of Religion and Revelation:
A Girardian Hermeneutic

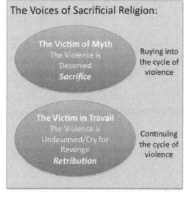

The Voices of Sacrificial Religion:

The Victim of Myth
The Violence is
Deserved
Sacrifice

Buying into
the cycle of
violence

The Victim in Travail
The Violence is
Undeserved/Cry for
Revenge
Retribution

Continuing
the cycle of
violence

The Voice of Revelation:

The Gospel Victim
The Violence is
Forgiven
Forgiveness

Ending
the cycle of
violence

© Michael Hardin
www.preachingpeace.org

One can only read the Bible sacrificially if one reads from a religious perspective, presupposing a Janus-faced god. The moment one recognizes that there are two distinct voices and furthermore that the voice of God is identified in only one of those voices—namely that of the forgiving victim—then the Bible is read not only from its own internal trajectory or hermeneutic, it also provides plenty of data for mimetic theory and the consequences of that data for Christian theology. To read the Bible this way is to a) read the text *sub theologia crucis*, b) to read non-sacrificially, c) to engage in what Dietrich Bonhoeffer called "a hermeneutics from below," d) to read anthropologically and e) to read scientifically.

To read the biblical text *sub theologia crucis* is to acknowledge the cross of Jesus as our *arche* ("beginning") or our *episteme* ("the method and source of knowing"). To read the Bible non-sacrificially is to read following the Bible's own internal hermeneutic, establishing the character of God as non-retributive and forgiving. Bonhoeffer's plea that the times required learning to read and hear from below has been fulfilled abundantly, particularly as theology is engaged by voices other than the until recently dominant white Eurocentric male. To read the Bible anthropologically is to read it with no intention of seeking the voice of God, but to mine it as literature that testifies to the same phenomena that archeology, myth, and ritual testify, namely the problem of sacred violence. Finally, to read the Bible in this fashion is to read it scientifically and one is able to show the true genius of the biblical text as well as that within the text that is its core, its shining light, its heart that is the love of Abba for the world demonstrated in the Forgiving one on Calvary. As Simone Weil puts it, "in the Gospel there is a theory of humanity" (this was one of Girard's favorite sayings).

In my book *The Jesus Driven Life,* I sought to work out the parameters of that anthropology, that "theory of humanity" found in the Gospel. I contend that Jesus' favorite self-designation, *bar enasha* (Aramaic), *ben adam* (Hebrew), *ho huios tou anthropou* (Greek), which Walter Wink has conclusively shown is to be understood as "The Human Being," is the starting place to begin to unpack the trajectory of this "True Human." Apart from all the debates it is surely the case that the Johannine "son of man," the Logos become flesh, is the one perfected on the cross. The import of the *tetelestai* ("It is completed/finished") of John 19:30 must be understood with reference to the *en arche* ("In the beginning") of John 1:1. The completion of the creation occurs on the cross! Jesus, the True Human dies and it is this cruciform spirit that he exhales over the world. Of course, a similar case can be made for the eschatological "son of man" sayings in the Gospels, once the antecedents of Second Temple Jewish retributive eschatology are removed. The eschatological "son of man" in the Gospels is the vindicated true human, not a bringer of divine wrath. Further engagement of this theme can be found in the Christ-Adam parallelism of the apostle Paul found in Romans 5 and 1 Corinthians 15 but has at its foundation the hymn embedded in Philippians (2:5–11). In all three cases, Jesus (in the Synoptic tradition), the Fourth Evangelist, and Paul all share a common understanding of the relationship between two anthropologies: one brings death and the other brings life. The former is the anthropology that we can talk about scientifically— that is, the one that brings death.

We will postpone examining the implications of the latter Jesucentric anthropology for ethics and spirituality to the final chapter. Prior to that we will explore two key Protestant doctrines, atonement and eschatology, in light of the mimetic theory. However, before we undertake these explorations the rest of this chapter will be taken up with framing a view of the authority of Scripture. This will be done apart from any theory of inspiration or canonization. The Bible neither is the Word of God nor does it become the Word of God. The work of the Spirit is to open our eyes to the cruciform lens we must use if we are to read the Bible, recognizing our sacrificial self-deceptive tendencies and listening attentively to the challenge and call to follow Jesus who alone is the Word of God. Discerning the two perspectives (but three voices) within Scripture can only come as revelation from the Crucified Forgiving Victim.

Of all the texts found in Holy Scripture, Girard professes to a canon within a canon and esteems the Passion

Narrative above all other texts.[4] It is the illuminating text for it is from the perspective of the innocent or random victim of a scapegoating process. In all four Gospel Passion Narratives, Jesus is portrayed as innocent.[5] The Gospels openly aver what myths have always sought to hide: the community is guilty, the victim is innocent. Originary myths and founding murder myths—the most foundational of myths, and the frame by which we humans would come to tell the story of our creation—is shown to be a horrible illusion in the trial and execution of Jesus of Nazareth. Even though Girard first thought that the mimetic theory was his "discovery" as he began composing *Things Hidden* he realized that "the origins of mimetic theory are wholly to be found in the biblical texts, old and new."[6]

The Passion Narrative is revelatory of two things and both of them are part of Girard's scientific anthropology.[7]

4. The following several pages are adapted from Chapter 3 of my PhD dissertation, *Must God be Violent?: Religion and Revelation in Karl Barth and René Girard.*

5. Burton Mack has an opposing opinion on this subject with reference to the Gospel of Mark in *The Myth of Innocence*. In light of the work done by Richard Bauckham on second-Temple "heavenly mediators" in *Jesus and the God of Israel*, and the work done on Paul's Christology by Chris Tilling in *Paul's Divine Christology*, I think the argument for the mythic Paul of the Hellenistic gospel (and his alleged influence) can be put to rest. If Gert Theissen's thesis that the Passion Narrative was framed during the Gaian crisis of 40–41 CE (*The Gospels in Context*), then one has at least three points of reference away from an argument that relies too heavily on a speculative history of social constructions and Ur-texts. If the early Christians believed Jesus had been raised from the dead, exalted to the right hand of majesty, and had been given the Unpronounceable Name (*Ha Shem*), they would have had a "high" Christology from early on.

6. Girard, *The One By Whom Scandal Comes*, 49.

7. Girard's reply to Schwager, *Correspondence*, (April 17 1978):

The first has to do with the Passion Narrative as ritual; Jesus' execution wasn't the first for the Romans as others had accusations prosecuted against them by the Jewish authorities from time to time according to Josephus. Jesus' death is one in a sequence of sacrificial social victims. It is not *sui generis* in this respect. The second has to do with myth: Jesus' execution exposes the foundation of Roman and Jewish culture and by extension back through history ("from Abel to Zechariah, son of Barachiah," Matt 23:34–35), all human culture, in violence and vengeance. It is *sui generis* in this sense. The human species has spilled a lot of blood, a lot of innocent blood. The dots from Jesus' crucifixion to mythology have always been there as we have been reminded by the *Religionsgeschichtliche Schule*; how those dots are connected and the consequent picture they project is the move Girard has made beyond the Bultmannian school.

The link between myth and gospel is not cosmology but the victim from whom ritual slaughter cosmology and language will emerge. Revelation is purely anthropological, just as Bultmann requires (even as he utilizes Heidegger's philosophy). However, this revelation is not merely a corrective to out-of-date worldviews or cosmologies. Instead it has to do with deception. The cross reveals the deception of myth; that is its revelatory function, perhaps, one could even say, its purpose inasmuch as "For anthropological truth to be unveiled, the Cross was necessary."[8]

"I think the essential in this book [*Things Hidden*] is to show that the sudden apparition of what I call the *transcendence over* asserts itself from the reading of the texts, and from this reading only. It is never, for my part, an *a priori*, or perhaps arbitrary position, a false superiority from which one would be hovering over reality."

8. Girard, *The One By Whom Scandal Comes*, 60.

By juxtaposing the Passion Narrative with the victim of myth, Girard has placed his finger on myth's dirty little secret, its hidden victims. Again, the Passion Narrative has the exact same elements one finds in myths or persecution texts as mentioned above: "a generalized loss of differences (the first stereotype), crimes that 'eliminate differences' (the second stereotype), and whether the identified authors of these crimes possess the marks that suggest a victim, the paradoxical marks of the absence of difference (the third stereotype)." Violence is the fourth stereotype. The Gospel is structured exactly like myth in order to deconstruct the lie of myth, the lie of human religion and culture, the lie of the principalities and the powers that violence and the sacred belong together. The Gospel separates them as far as east is from west. Girard, for example, compares the story of Joseph in Genesis with that of Oedipus:

> It is not just the Oedipus myth that is contradicted by the Joseph narrative, but the very structure of myths themselves. The myth always asks the question, "Is he guilty?" and provides the answer: "Yes." Jocasta and Laios are right to expel Oedipus, since he will commit parricide and incest. Yes, Thebes is right to do the same, since Oedipus has committed parricide and incest. The mythical narrative always confirms that the heroes are guilty. In the case of Joseph, everything works in reverse. The hero is wrongly accused. The question is the same, but the answer opens our eyes to an entirely different world. I think there is a fundamental opposition between biblical texts and myths. The truth of the biblical text isn't a question of referentiality/non-referentiality. It doesn't have to be referential to be true. It is true in so far as

> it is *the denial of the myths,* which are the source
> of the lie, since they always confirm the scape-
> goat mechanism, and in so doing cover it up.[9]

Revelation in Girard's reading of the Bible is the revelation of the non-retributive character of God (which exposes the retributive character of humans) and this is precisely what religion cannot welcome, for religion requires an angry (at a minimum) or a Janus-faced (at a maximum) deity. Revelation in Girard has a relational reconciliatory ground (just as it does in Barth) with epistemic, ethical, and soteriological implications. Revelation is grounded in two very important realities. First, revelation is cruciform in character, that is, the Passion Narrative is structured as myth and subversively exposes the failed unanimity required for the scapegoating mechanism to operate; second, revelation is of the character of God as forgiving, thus establishing an alternative shape of community formation and identity.

The Gospel, in other words, completely deconstructs the Janus-faced god by showing that the two sides of this god are not attributes of love and justice (or wrath), but are two distinct streams blended together thus obscuring revelation with religion. By separating these two streams we may once and for all separate violence and the sacred. "God is non-violent" is another way of saying "God is love."

It is the innocent victim that is the common ground of both the human sciences and theology. If the human quest for intellectual foundations has been going on since time immemorial and if modernity thought it acquired a foundation in rational logical thought abstracted from the realities of life, and if post-Shoah awareness that language

9. Girard, *Evolution and Conversion,* 200.

is "power-laden," and further if all of our attempts to lo-
cate a foundation are doomed to collapse because we have
not yet acknowledged the one foundation upon which
we build and from which we derive knowledge—namely,
the scapegoat—then the intellectual crisis of our time
makes perfect sense. The innocent victim "that which
the builders rejected" is the only foundation upon which
human knowledge has ever been grounded. Postmoder-
nity's attempt to localize all potentially universalizing
meta-narratives has created a situation where we must
share our insights across disciplines, boundaries, and all
forms of tribalism—academic or social. The one thing we
all have in common is that the very vast majority of us
have been or are involved in negative mimetic relations
and scapegoating; a smaller percentage have been those
scapegoats—for instance, scientists, housewives, farmers,
teachers, sailors, abused childrens, refugees of war, persons of other faith traditions or ethnic backgrounds, and
the LGBTQ community. Real knowledge is going to have
to begin with the innocent victim and the scapegoat; this
is the transforming effect of the divine *logos* (or "divine
virus" as Anthony Bartlett puts it) on our epistemology
and our semiotics and our hermeneutics as well.[10]

The victim is the "tacit dimension"[11] of all knowledge. This is why beginning all Christian theology *sub
theologia crucis* and working everything out from this
point is essential if it is to be Christian theology and if it is
to be designated as "revelation." It is also the starting point
for secular anthropology when mimetic theory is used as
a discipline. It is the same knowledge being worked out

10. On epistemology see James Alison, *The Joy of Being Wrong*;
on semiotics see Anthony Bartlett, *Virtually Christian*, and on
hermeneutics see my *The Jesus Driven Life*.

11. The term is taken from Michael Polanyi.

in both spheres, both frames of reference. If theology and science were to adopt such a position, the ethical implications alone would be staggering. In other words there need be no bifurcation between theology and the human sciences if the starting point is the epistemology of the scapegoat or "the intelligence of the victim" (James Alison). If the sciences of humanity and theology wish to have a mutually satisfying relationship they will both excavate from the ruins of sacred violence.

By approaching the Bible anthropologically we are able to see that its effects are best understood when *we allow the Bible to read itself as it reads mythology.* That is, when we come to the text with no presumption as to its divine character, the very thing that held our religion together (*religio* = to bind), namely a sacrificial (mythological) hermeneutic, is exposed within the pages of the Bible, over and over and over again. In case we didn't get it reading the Jewish scriptures it is given in living color four times in the Gospel Passion Narratives. If we still don't get it, it is also found in Paul, particularly 2 Corinthians 3. One also finds it in the sermon to the Hebrews. As we read the Bible as it reads mythology, the veil of deception is lifted from our faces and we can see truth where before we only saw deception and confusion. This is the anthropological power of the Bible and it requires no theory of inspiration. In fact, it is far superior to any view of the Bible as inerrant or infallible in that it does not spend its time in cheap apologetics or become bogged down in scholastic minutiae nor does it ignore all of the internal contradictions. In fact, the contradictions are precisely the key to understanding the Bible. Hearkening back to the previous chapter we may thoughtfully engage the Bible using "content-criticism" because the writers, editors, and copyists are doing precisely that!

Undoubtedly there are those who will say that we are cherry-picking the Bible. Technically such is not the case as we are contending that all texts must be interpreted; no text is tossed aside as so much cultural baggage, whether in liberal superiority or conservative dispensationalism. We can easily avoid the wax nose of Scripture by always acknowledging our starting point, the cross which brings a new *logos* ("message"); again, this *logos*/logic is "the intelligence of the victim." The Bible makes an important contribution to scientific anthropology, just as scientific anthropology validates the insights of a mimetic appropriation of the Bible, indeed of all literature. In other words, our theory of revelation, our epistemology, our hermeneutic, and our source of authority are all one and the same thing: Jesus Christ crucified.

The implications of this are, of course, staggering for now the Bible is displaced from the matrix of religion as a magical text and allowed to speak freely to any religious project that muzzles it. A mimetic interpretation completes the anti-idolatrous project of the Hebrew prophets as well as Barth's project of ridding Protestantism of its religious theological idols and Bonhoeffer's search for a "non-religious interpretation of Christian concepts." A mimetic interpretation, because it does not begin with a presupposition about divinity, finds itself with the advantage of allowing the biblical trajectory of revelation to create a proper understanding of the divine through the lens of "Christ crucified."

DISCUSSION QUESTIONS:

1. What were you taught about the nature, content, and transmission of the biblical texts? How much of what you were taught has little or no basis in historical reality?

2. Pick any conquest story from the book of Joshua and seek to read it in terms of the voice of the victim(s).

3. What would you tell someone who asked about the relation of the Bible to mythology?

4. Is "the intelligence of the victim" strong enough to provide hermeneutical support for interpreting Scripture?

5

ATONEMENT AND ESCHATOLOGY

WE ARE NOW IN a position to begin applying all we have learned to this business of the death of Jesus or atonement. We will see where the default position of Protestantism has merged violence and the sacred and how the anti-sacrificial trajectory begun in the Jewish writings is carried through in understanding Jesus' death in significant portions of early Christianity. If—following Paul, the Evangelists, Luther, Moltmann, and Girard—we engage in an anti-sacrificial reading of the Bible, knowing that we have been using the mythological reading up until now, where we identified with the persecuting, violence justifying, scapegoating sacrificial mob, then we will engage the exact texts enjoined by the sacrificial reading and provide an alternative, more internally coherent hermeneutic.

We shall proceed by first framing the Protestant default position on the doctrine of atonement. Then we shall look at this doctrine through the lens of mimetic theory.

Third, having established two ways of reading atonement texts, we shall engage in several examples from the New Testament. We will conclude our discussion of atonement with some summary remarks on what an anti-sacrificial view of the death of Jesus suggests and entails, particularly as it relates to ethics and spirituality. Having armed ourselves with this hermeneutic we shall then explore the role and function of the doctrine of eternal conscious torment or "hell." While I believe that there is just cause for a sacrificial reading of the Bible, inasmuch as the Bible contains sacrificial material, this type of reading is unable to see how the non-sacrificial Gospel is explicitly set over against this type of hermeneutic and so mingles all texts and buries revelation under an avalanche of religion.

Even that, however, is not enough to stop the Gospel from breaking free time and again, as it has done throughout the history of Christendom. The challenge to the hegemonic character of the default position on the atonement is only threatening because Christian believers have been told that a sacrificial rendering of the death of Jesus *is the Gospel* and to disbelieve the sacrificial view is tantamount to losing one's salvation. In other words the Church has tied salvation to a hermeneutic. What is being accepted by the person on the street who gets "born again" is a hermeneutic; it is a poor hermeneutic, to be sure, but whatever it is *it is not the Gospel.* The apostolic Gospel is the exact opposite of the Protestant default position.

A quick overview of atonement theory would note that the Christus Victor theory held sway for about the first 1,100 years of church history. This view stressed Jesus' victory over the principalities and the powers, the satan, death, and hades. It would produce several different versions. One more objectionable form, which has God bribing the devil, was taken to task by Anselm of Canterbury who shifted the metaphoric background of atonement from a military campaign to that of a courtroom. In 1098 *Cur Deus Homo?* was published and from that point on the West would be saddled with a doctrine of atonement that used medieval metaphors of power relations (lord/serf). It was in the mid-sixteenth century that John Calvin would shift the metaphor once again to the juridical by taking Anselm's feudal categories and translating them into those of the Judge and the Accused. This move by John Calvin (in the late 1530s) totally transformed the Gospel and completely dressed it in archaic sacrificial clothing. Calvin's view of atonement is hugely important not just for its failure, but for the incredible mass deception it has foisted on modernity.

In Calvin's view, known as penal substitutionary atonement or PSA, God the Father righteously pours divine wrath out on Jesus as he is dying. Jesus is the sacrifice for our sins. God required justice (an economy of exchange) using the logic of Anselm and Calvin. More so, divine justice when divinely offended meant that a temporal creature could not pay an eternal debt thus it required the divine to pay that debt, ergo the Son becomes flesh, fulfills the Law perfectly, as the obedient covenant-partner of God, and takes upon himself the just wrath of God against all human sin. In this atonement paradigm the Son becomes a perfect sacrifice thus appeasing the Father who is then able to love a portion of humanity again. This is the default position preached Sunday after Sunday in hundreds of thousands of churches across America.

It is true that certain Evangelical theologians have sought to nuance this view. The two most successful attempts were by the Scottish preacher John McLeod

Campbell in nineteenth-century Scotland and Karl Barth in twentieth-century Switzerland. Neither Campbell's nor Barth's rendering of Jesus' death requires the limited atonement associated with Reformed Orthodoxy and both are stingingly critical of the God needing to be propitiated in the crass manner of neo-Calvinism or Billy Graham. Nevertheless even Barth ultimately falls prey to the need to "balance the scales" of divine justice and so there is an element of an economy of exchange in his view of Jesus' death, particularly in *Church Dogmatics IV/1*.

It was not God who created economies of exchange, it was we humans and it originates in the substitution of the innocent victim for the group. It is better that one die than the group perish. God is beyond all economies of exchange, for economies of exchange are the opposite of grace. Economies of exchange require reciprocity; grace gives because it is grace and knows no other way of relating. Grace expects nothing in return even as it hopes for hospitality.

One of the current forms this discussion takes can be found in the work of Douglas Campbell. In his massive book, *The Deliverance of God,* Campbell makes an almost exhausting case that Paul's letter to the Romans consists of both Pauline texts and "texts" or "voices" of the false teacher. However he is perhaps better known for his criticism of the soteriological default position which he calls "methodological Arianism." Following the work of James Torrance on covenants and contracts, Campbell argues that contemporary Reformed and Evangelical theology says covenant but really means contract. Scottish Reformed theologian T.F. Torrance (following McLeod Campbell) and Doug Campbell argue that redemption is initiated, culminated, and brought to fruition by God and

God alone. Covenants in this view are unilateral. However, default Protestant soteriology has turned them into contracts in which both parties have promises and obligations. With this we are back into medieval, if not archaic, metaphors and economies of exchange.

Economies of exchange are, as we saw in Chapter 2, grounded in mimetic reciprocity. When someone invites you to dinner you don't think of going empty-handed. Perhaps you stop at the bakery for a savory treat or bring a nice flower arrangement or bottle of wine. Why do people do this? In archaic society it was known as the "potlatch"; in modern times it is called Christmas. Economies of exchange are part and parcel of the sacrificial mechanism, or what you get when you join violence and the sacred. The first and most important thing this view does is to make God a rival. And herein lies the presenting issue in all sacrificial atonement theories. If God is our rival all we end up with is a doctrine of God where God has a love-hate relationship with us, where if you do the right thing you are rewarded and if you do the wrong thing you are doomed. Call it fate, call it karma, call it balance, call it god. Call it whatever you want. It is all the same thing: a Janus-faced god. And the only way a Janus-faced god knows how to make atonement is with sacrifice. I wish to briefly bring three arguments to bear on this.

Independent scholar Anthony Bartlett's dissertation, *Cross Purposes,* dismantled Anselm's concept of substitution arguing that the metaphors for atonement that Anselm drew upon reflected the environment of medieval feudalism and not biblical usage. Referencing Girard, Derrida, and biblical studies, Bartlett argued that the substitutionary mechanism proposed by Anselm depended upon the hierarchy of feudal society. This resulted in atonement being framed as an economy of exchange. Honor as a social commodity became a theological category. Undermining the logic of Anselm's concept of the necessity of sacrifice, Bartlett demonstrates convincingly that economies of exchange cannot be part of a Christian theory of the atoning work of Jesus.

Second, Mark Heim, in his excellent *Saved from Sacrifice,* examines the Bible from this dual trajectory theory of religion and revelation, where there are two voices in the Bible, that of the persecutory myth-making mob and that of the victim. He argues that if God were to reveal God's self as God and as different from all human gods and theologies (idols), the only way this could be done is by taking either the side of the persecuting community—which would bring nothing to revelation and simply establish religion—or to take the side of the victim. From Judah and Joseph to Jesus and Stephen the voice of God has always been heard in the forgiving victim. Heim says,

> God enters into the position of the victim of sacrifice (a position already defined by human practice) and occupies it so as to be able to act from that place to reverse sacrifice and redeem us from it. God steps forward in Jesus to be one subject to the human practice of atonement in blood, not because that is God's preferred logic or because this itself it God's aim, but because this is the very site where human bondage and sin are enacted.[1]

In a most ironic twist it can be said that adherents of the substitutionary theory of the atonement, in at least its variety of Evangelical versions, run into a major problem. The narrative shape they give to the death of Jesus is

1. Heim, *Saved from Sacrifice,* 143.

that of the mythmaking mob, not the narrative as told by the victim. Indeed, Mark Heim warns us that it is Pilate and Herod who have a sacrificial interpretation of Jesus' death and that, "the gospels make it clear that it is Jesus' antagonists who view his death as a redemptive sacrifice, one life given for many . . . Here is a caution for Christian theology. We must beware that in our reception and interpretation of the Gospel we do not end up entering the passion story on the side of Jesus' murderers."[2]

In *Saved from Sacrifice*, Heim uses mimetic theory to show that the two perspectives, that of the persecutor and that of the victim, are the means by which to distinguish sacrificial renderings of the death of Jesus from non-sacrificial ones. Heim makes several important points. First, the *dei* ("necessity"), of the death of Jesus, found in the Synoptic tradition, is not that of divine necessity. The Father has absolutely no need for the Son to die, does not will it, nor desire it. Second, Heim views the cross through the three fold lens of "The Cross no one Sees," "The Cross We Can't Forget," and "The Cross that Faith Keeps Empty," each corresponding to the invisible victim of sacrifice, the scapegoat, and the vindicated victim of mimetic theory. Heim has also contributed to the debates around iconography of the death of Jesus in the early church demonstrating that there is pictorial evidence of Jesus' death as a 'lynching.'

Third, I have argued in several essays that the death of Jesus has nothing to do with atoning God; God does not need, desire or want sacrifice. In *The Jesus Driven Life* I showed how various sayings in the Synoptic tradition, Paul and the Fourth Gospel in relation to atonement, which are used as warrants for sacrificial atonement

2. Ibid., 125–26.

theories, could legitimately be exegeted non-sacrificially. Texts include Psalm 22, Rom 3:23–26, Mark 10:45 and 2 Cor 5:21. In order to demonstrate the fecundity of the mimetic theory for interpreting such texts here are two examples from that book.[3]

What is the relation of God to Jesus as he is dying? For many, God is in heaven as Jesus dies on earth and God is pouring wrath or anger out on Jesus. God must do this because God has placed our sins on Jesus and God deals with sin by exercising wrath. Some point out that even Jesus believed this when he quotes Psalm 22 from the cross "My God, my God, why have you forsaken me?" God could only forsake Jesus if he had turned his back on our sin (or so the logic goes).

Jesus' quotation of Psalm 22 is the only time in the gospels where Jesus does not refer to God as Father, so we must ask what is occurring here. Most of us are familiar with Psalm 23 and could recite it by heart. It brings us comfort in times of distress. But perhaps we are not so familiar with Psalm 22.

Psalm 22 is a cry of dereliction. It is a psalm about the experience of being the victim of an unjust accusation and of being prosecuted. In short, it is a psalm about being a scapegoat. Many of us have experienced this: we have been part of a group that has generated rumors about us that we knew were not true. One by one our friends took the side of the group against us until we were standing alone and no longer part of the group. It is a horrible experience.

When Jesus quotes Psalm 22, he is seeking to remind his executioners that they are playing the role of

---

3. The next several pages are adapted from *The Jesus Driven Life*.

the scapegoating community. If someone were to quote the opening line of Psalm 23, "The Lord is my shepherd," most of us could go on and recite a good portion of that psalm. By quoting the opening line of Psalm 22, Jesus is not saying that God has abandoned him; he is bringing to mind the entire context of the psalm. One might object that this is not necessarily the case but it is important to note that breathing was very difficult on a cross and extended conversations and dialogues would have been both very painful and virtually impossible.

But that is not all. Psalm 22 is a psalm of vindication. At the end the psalmist knows that "God is not far off" and that "God has not hidden his face." The psalmist knows that God has neither "despised nor disdained the suffering of the afflicted one." Ultimately Psalm 22 is a cry of hope. The Jews who heard Jesus cry the first words of Psalm 22 from the cross heard not only the sense of abandonment, but also the hope, because they knew that psalm! This hope is reflected in all of the passion predictions of Jesus who, knowing he will suffer at the hands of an angry mob still believes, in spite of everything, that God will deliver him by vindicating his innocence. For Jesus, as for the psalmist, God is not some far off angry deity. It is the crowd who is angry, and the crowd who requires sacrifice of the innocent. God is caring and present with the victim.

A final point of the recitation of Psalm 22 from the crucified Jesus is a theological one: unlike the belief of the mob and the Jewish leaders that they are doing God a favor in getting rid of the troublemaker Jesus, the use of Psalm 22 is an indication that God does not authorize humanity's sacrifice of Christ. God is not seen as the actor who sacrifices His Son; rather, this sacrificial death is one that God rejects. Thus God is "absent" (as agent), not "present," in our sacrificial processes.

So far I have sought to head off at the pass two major objections to a wide spread misunderstanding of God as Father. The first is that Father is to be perceived in power terms and the second is that God was angry with Jesus as he hung dying. I have also suggested that by beginning with the cross of Jesus in our understanding of God we can see that God's relationship to Jesus must be conceived in terms other than those we have been given in our dominant theological traditions.

When, at his baptism (Mark 1:9–11), God says to Jesus that "You are my beloved son," we should not suppose that anything ever changed in Jesus' relationship to his *Abba*. If there is one constant we can rely on in our theology it is that the relationship between Jesus and God never changed. This is why (and it can get complicated) it is so important to begin our Christian understanding of the Trinitarian God from the perspective of the cross. If God is two-faced—if he is both loving, evidenced at Jesus' baptism and transfiguration, and later at the point of the cross, angry with Jesus—then we have a pagan, and therefore idolatrous, view of God. The gods of paganism were a blend of human characteristics both good and bad. Some say that we must hold things like God's love and wrath, or God's mercy and holiness in tension. If God is Janus-faced this is true. Janus is the god of the double face. But an authentic understanding of the Father/Son relationship does away with any tension. If our god is tense, maybe he needs to see a psychiatrist!

Let's look at another well-known passage, Rom 3:23–26:

> For all have sinned and fall short of the glory
> of God, and are justified freely by his grace
> through the redemption that came by Christ
> Jesus. God presented him as a sacrifice of
> atonement [*hilasterion*], through faith in his
> blood. He did this to demonstrate his justice,
> because in his forbearance he had left the sins
> committed beforehand unpunished— he did it
> to demonstrate his justice at the present time,
> so as to be just and the one who justifies those
> who have faith in Jesus.

There are several key questions we must resolve in order to interpret this text. The first concerns the translation of *hilasterion*, which the NIV translates as "a sacrifice of atonement." The KJV translates this term as "propitiation" while the RSV uses "expiation." To propitiate a god is to make a sacrifice to appease wrath, anger, or a curse. We are already familiar with this as the sacrificial principle. On the other hand, to expiate sin is to remove it; it looks to the object causing sin rather than God as the object to be appeased. There has been quite a bit of ink spilled over which translation best captures *hilasterion*. Those who reject an angry divinity prefer expiation while others, such as neo-Reformed thinkers John Piper and Thomas Schreiner, believe that God's wrath needs to be assuaged and justice satisfied and thus prefer propitiation.

The way out of this dilemma is to follow the logic of Paul's subversion of the sacrificial process. Robert Hamerton-Kelly points out that,

> The major new element is that Paul inverts
> the traditional understanding of sacrifice so
> that God is the offerer, not the receiver, and
> the scapegoat goes into the sacred precinct
> rather than out of it. Christ is a divine offering

to humankind, not a human offering to God. In the normal order of sacrifice, humans give and the god receives; here the god gives and humans receive. The usual explanation of this passage is that human sin deserved divine punishment, but in mercy God substituted a propitiatory offering to bear the divine wrath instead of humanity. We must insist on the fact that the recipients are human, otherwise we fall into the absurdity of God's giving a propitiatory gift to God. The second point to note is that not only the order of giver and receiver is reversed but also the spatial order. Normally the offerer goes from profane to sacred space to make the offering; here the offerer comes out of sacred space into profane, publically to set forth (*proetheto*) the propitiation (*hilasterion*) there. These inversions of the normal order of sacrifice mean that it is not God who needs to be propitiated, but humanity, and not in the recesses of the Sacred, but in the full light of day.[4]

The point of this is that if one insists on translating *hilasterion* as propitiation then one must also take into consideration the subversion of the sacrificial principle. There is therefore, in this passage no justification for arguing that God's wrath must be propitiated. We humans are the ones who need to be appeased. Whether we translate *hilasterion* as "propitiation" or "expiation," in neither case do we need speak of God's wrath being appeased, it is not in the text itself, it can only come from prior assumptions regarding sacrifice in general.

4. Hamerton-Kelly, *Sacred Violence*, 80. See also the (virtually) exhaustive exegesis on this passage by Campbell, *Deliverance*, 601–714.

With the deconstruction of the religious or sacrificial reading how does mimetic theory help frame the doctrine of the atonement? First, just as there are two types of mimesis—negative or rivalrous mimesis and positive or restorative mimesis—so, by addressing the principalities and the powers as is done in the Christus Victor theory, mimetic theory recognizes it is dealing with negative mimesis and its effects, including the founding and maintenance of religion and civilization. Second, mimetic theory, combined with research from various disciplines of moral theory and cognitive studies, uses Abelard's *moral influence* theory of the atonement, which stresses God as a model of love. LeRon Schults has done groundbreaking research in rehabilitating Abelard and the moral influence theory of the atonement in light of contemporary science.[5] He collapses the false distinction between objective and subjective models of at-one-ment by outlining the objective effects of subjective change in interdividual human subjectivity. This focus offers the possibility of seeing the death of Christ as the ground for a new anthropology, one of positive or healing mimesis.

There are many other things we can say about a positive mimetic reading of the death of Jesus, some of which we will explore in the next chapter as we look at the death of Jesus as model for spirituality and discipleship.[6]

We must, however, continue our journey regarding the death of Jesus, which in the default position saves us from burning like eternal toast. In a few pages I will sketch some objections to the traditional sacrificial view

5. Shults, *Ethics*; See also my essay *Practical Implications*.

6. One important element the Church needs are new atonement hymns that reflect a non-sacrificial hermeneutic. Mark Heim has composed a beautiful example in his "No More of This" at http://preachingpeace.org/images/No_More_Of_This.pdf

of eschatological judgement, and offer some views on an alternative non-sacrificial or compassionate eschatology. The default position holds that heaven and hell are two opposing destinies for human souls after death. The former is given as a reward, the latter as punishment.

There are several objections that can be raised against the traditional view.[7]

First, the doctrine of eternal punishment is nothing other than an eschatological economy of exchange as Sharon Baker-Putt has argued in *Razing Hell*. Baker had already noted the problem of economies of exchange in atonement in her PhD dissertation and seeks to deconstruct the default position of eschatological judgment contending that in the Bible, God's justice is restorative not retributive. That is, she follows the trajectory of revelation reading eschatological texts *sub theologia* crucis. In contrast to the trajectory of religion, which reads eschatological judgment texts as actually involving divine or satanic punishment, Baker argues that the mercy of God knows no limits or boundaries because it knows no economy of exchange.

Second, Jesus did not share the Second Temple Jewish view of the afterlife found in I Enoch and other apocalyptic literature (e.g., the Psalms of Solomon, the Dead Sea Scrolls, etc). Brad Jersak has convincingly demonstrated that Jesus did not have a dualistic doctrine of the afterlife but spoke only of Gehenna, which was used as a prophetic metaphor of judgment on sacrificial violence especially as found in the prophet Jeremiah, that fierce and trenchant critic of the first Jewish Temple. In *Her Gates Will Never Be Shut*, Jersak exegetes the Bible and shows that the

7. An excellent teaching tool that examines the traditional view of Christian hell is the documentary *Hellbound?* Information can be found at www.hellboundthemovie.com.

eschatological perspective held by the Eastern churches legitimately tends toward universalism.[8] One of Jersak's favorite examples is that of orthodox Christian universalist Gregory of Nyssa, editor of the second revised creed of Nicaea (Nicene-Constantinopolitan Creed of 381 CE). Rather than being a fringe or heretical doctrine, Christian eschatologies that are universalistic in hope and restorationist in character have a long and storied pedigree in Christian history. Eschatology need not have an implicit economy of exchange any more than atonement.

Third, hell has a history. The doctrine of hell did not come dropped from the heavens by God. Alan Bernstein has shown that dualistic doctrines of the afterlife have their origins in antiquity but are given a structured theology by Zoroaster in Persia eight centuries before Jesus.[9] This Iranian worldview entered Judaism through the Jewish exile of the priesthood and aristocracy in Babylon, gained traction in Judaism following the Hellenization of Palestine around 300 BCE and came to full flower in and around the Maccabean revolt in 167 BCE in collections like I Enoch or books like Daniel. This was certainly not the only eschatology on the second Temple Jewish scene, the Sadducees had no eschatology to speak of for example. Christianity begins to develop the doctrine of hell in the early Middle Ages as a place of torment and by the time humanity reaches the high Middle Ages, Dante has carved out a place for every type of sinner in his hell. Milton assured Protestants that if they did not behave they would surely end up weeping and wailing and gnashing their teeth forever. Protestant soteriology is absolutely beholden to both Second Temple Jewish apocalyptic and

8. Jersak, *Her Gates Will Never Be Shut.*

9. Bernstein, *The Formation of Hell.*

medieval speculation on the afterlife. The general public, unaware of all this research data, continues to live in fear of eternal torment and a god who accuses.

Fourth, in addition to Bernstein's history of the doctrine of hell, Jeffrey Burton Russell has composed a corresponding history of *The Prince of Darkness*. Russell traces the history of the personification of evil from the archaic devil to the Christian satan and from there to the medieval Lucifer and the modern Mephistopheles.[10] Just like the doctrine of hell so also the doctrine of the [so-called] ruler of hell has a history. Both of these histories put to the lie the argument that "the Bible contains a doctrine of eternal conscious torment." It does and it doesn't. It does inasmuch as it has texts which share the worldview of I Enoch; it doesn't in that we can see the apostolic church engaging in a hard re-boot of their eschatology. One can see this especially in Paul from whom we have a series of letters. We can trace Paul's developing eschatology from his earliest authentic letters to his last. Following Campbell and arguing for an early date (41 CE), in I and II Thessalonians, Paul is still in the grip of a second Temple eschatology.[11] However after his break with the Jerusalem church at Antioch in 48 and prior to his flurry of letter writing between 50–52 Paul has rethought his entire eschatological framework. It has now been thought through *sub theologia crucis* and the Adam-Christ typology serves as both a protology and an eschatology for Paul. The creation-wide implication of Jesus' atonement can be seen in the citation of the hymn in Col 1:15–20 composed

10. See references to Jeffrey Burton Russell's five books in the bibliography.

11. Campbell, *Framing Paul*, offers the most convincing Pauline chronology to date, surpassing even the excellent work of Jewett and Hurd.

in mid-50. Thus, Paul can take the Adam-Christ parallelism of Rom 5:12–21 and turn it into a theory of universal redemption for both Jew and Gentile, for everybody in Romans 11.

Paul's "conversion" from a sacrificial to a non-sacrificial approach is evidenced in his letters by comparing the Thessalonian correspondence to his later authentic letters. This ought to be warrant enough for us to abandon the default doctrine. Combined with Jesus' various utterances on Gehenna—which was primarily aimed at those who held to a retributive eschatology but who always managed to find themselves in heaven with God while other bad people burned in eternal flames—there is plenty of warrant for Christian theology to finally abandon the influence of Zoroaster, Enochic speculation, and medieval terror in its view of the afterlife.

A mimetic reading of eschatology does not necessarily preclude apocalypse but a mimetic theorist has options at this point. One can follow Girard who, in his last book *Battling to the End,* saw post 9/11 human history reverting back to sacrificial mechanisms. Because of the influence of the Gospel, this mechanism of exposing our propensity to victimage has undergone a slow but steady decay and now no longer works because of the viral infection of the Crucified. Human history thus has no safety mechanism with which to deal with escalating violence and so an apocalypse of our own making may well be in the works. Girard was not an optimist about the direction of human history when he died last year.

On the other hand, another eschatological vision grounded in a theology of the cross and its positive effects is possible. In *Virtually Christian,* Anthony Bartlett challenges the semiotics of Christian discourse that are embedded in human violence. The *logos* of the Gospel destructures and reconfigures the wisdom that is to be found in the abyss of human victimage, transforming retribution into forgiveness and individuality into community. The postmodern fascination with the "sign" is transfigured in the revelation of the originary victim, the scapegoat evidenced by Jesus' reference to "the sign of Jonah." Bartlett convincingly displaces much of the metaphysical discourse around Jesus with the language of relationality and love. In the long run a mimetic rendering of the death of Jesus and eschatology from a non-sacrificial perspective has greater claim to be authentic and orthodox good news than that of the Protestant default position with its Janus-faced god.

DISCUSSION QUESTIONS:

1. How important is it to have scientific understanding of sacrifice and the role of economies of exchange before reading the Bible? How has a lack of understanding distorted Christian doctrine?

2. In what ways does a mimetic rendering of the death of Jesus a) remove retribution from God, b) place the burden on humanity and c) show the character of God as forgiving/healing/redemptive?

3. What were you taught about afterlife and punishment? How have your views changed?

4. How does our doctrine of the afterlife affect our current ethics?

6

ETHICS AND
SPIRITUALITY

IN THIS CHAPTER WE want to ask the important "So
What?" question. Why does any of this matter? The mid-
second century epistle to Diognetus says "violence (*bia*)
is not an attribute of God." We have taken this counsel
to heart as we have looked briefly at some of the implications of removing retributive violence from the doctrines of God, Christology, soteriology, anthropology,
and eschatology. We have also examined our views on
epistemology, hermeneutics, and the Bible in the light of
separating violence and the sacred *sub theologia crucis*.
How does this play out in real life? We shall now turn to
what the Reformed tradition calls the Doctrine of The
Christian Life.

In *The Jesus Driven Life*, I looked at all three Synoptic
accounts of the great commandment and concluded that
in each case the two-fold great commandment was framed
either by the tradition or Jesus himself as a hermeneutic.

Love is a hermeneutic and the fact that the double commandment is not really double is evidenced by the recital of the opening of the Shema in Luke's text where God's oneness or wholeness is in an emphatic position. To read the Bible through the lens of the love of God and neighbor as one and the same thing is a sentiment also expressed in the Matthean parable of the sheep and goats (Matt 25:31–46) which culminates his five discourses. Spirituality and ethics are one and the same thing; they are just practiced in relation to different objects, in the one case God, in the other case the neighbor. While it is possible using form, redaction and literary tools to slice and dice the Sermon on the Mount to great benefit for historical interpretation, it is absolutely impossible to separate the spirituality and the ethics found in this discourse.

Girard did not do ethics, for ethics belongs to positive mimesis. Positive mimesis, which is indeed to be found in the historical Jesus of Nazareth, was simply not possible until after the vindication of the forgiving victim, when Jesus would be raised from the dead by the breath of God. Girard is very clear that the scientific character of the mimetic theory ends with the burial of Jesus. In *I See Satan,* Girard is also very clear that for him, "The Resurrection is not only a miracle, an enigma, a transgression of natural laws; it is a spectacular sign of the entrance into the world of a power superior to violent contagion."[1] What is this world? It is the world of a very creative, restorative, and healing mimesis.

The Risen Christ (*Christus Praesens*) brings the true eschatological word, "Shalom." In Shalom, all differences

1. Girard, *I See Satan*, 189. I have slightly altered the translation of James Williams ("La Résurrection n'est pas seulement miracle, prodige, transgression des lois naturelles . . . "), *Je Vois Satan Tomber*, 246.

are healed and all wrongs forgiven. The resurrection is the vindication of the True Human, the font of all new creation. However, according to Adrio König there is an "eclipse of Christ in eschatology."[2] John E. Phelan avers, "Everything done in the church is, or should be, done in light of the presence of the kingdom of God in Jesus' ministry, message, death and resurrection. The church's message, ministry and communal life are all given shape by the promise of resurrection and judgment, and the coming of the new heavens and new earth. Christians are a people of hope."[3] *The New York Times'* best-selling *Left Behind* series might make one a little less optimistic as to how many congregations preach and practice this in a holistic fashion. The default eschatological Christ of modern Christendom looks more like John Wayne, Chuck Norris, or the Terminator. The resurrection shalom has been exchanged for subjective religious piety in the privacy of one's heart. Instead of peace, fear rules. The more things change the more they stay the same.

If one were to survey the many and different types of Judaism in Jesus' time with respect to what life after death held, one would find that there were various views. One group, the Sadducees were Bible believers. If the Bible said it, then it was true. Only Torah is the Bible. The Torah does not talk about resurrection so there is no life after death. The prophetic writings contain a mixture of views—some are peaceful, others rather gory. Groups in Jesus' day that had an eschatology, a view of the end, all shared something in common. They all had a penal or retributive final judgment scene. This is true of the literature of the *perushim*, called separatists (Pharisees),

2. König, *The Eclipse of Christ in Eschatology*

3. Phelan, *Essential Eschatology.*

in the Gospels. Retributive eschatology is writ large in the Essene communities. It can be found in the Enochic literature and the priestly movement related to it. In this eschatology, the future is bleak and death is to be feared. In most scenarios only a few, the righteous, are saved.

However, Jesus' resurrection puts to rest the second Temple eschatology debates. Jesus' Easter *shalom* was not a way followers of Jesus could have envisioned themselves in relation to the justice of the future. As the clear dawn of a new day, the Old was old for the New had come. The New Shalom for All, the Day of Divine Mercy was God's trump card over darker end-time scenarios.

Thus in the resurrection encounter with Jesus, we experience in our present (even if the Christ event occurred in our past) what the future holds for all (which is the forgiveness of sins). When some preach that Jesus is coming back with wrath, they do not make the shift from a certain type of second Temple Jewish eschatology to God's eschatology. God comes to us as a merciful Judge in the resurrection. History is forgiven, space and time are redeemed. God has done this. The gospel is not about us, it is about God and what God has done for us. When those who believe in a wrathful eschatological deity say that it is important to "take ownership" of our salvation—that is, to believe in a certain set of theological propositions—then the problem is set up from the start. What is announced is exactly the opposite of gospel. The resurrection of Jesus must be marginalized in this view, no matter how strenuously some go right to apologetics when it comes to faith in the Risen Lord. In this way of thinking, the resurrection is merely the logical consequence of the crucifixion of Jesus, and Pentecost is an afterthought. Rational proofs are supposed to provide the power—they don't.

We noticed previously how the disciples were expecting a wrathful Judge at the end and how this was the default position of many Jews in Jesus' and Paul's day. What matters in the resurrection of Jesus is *how* the victim returns. This is all too often missing in the discussion about the resurrection of Jesus. Jesus embodies "shalom" in his coming. Jesus will always come as a peacemaker. Jesus' blood speaks a better word than that of Abel; that is the revelation in his blood, the cup we share in his name that brings forgiveness. This is the voice that stops all violence with the announcement of shalom.

Was Jesus about shalom in his lifetime? The Jesus who returns in the resurrection is the same Jesus who was crucified ("See my scars."). How is the crucified portrayed in the Gospels? Look at those he cared for, how he cared for them. Look at those he blessed and called blessed. Look at those he healed, freed from bondage, enlightened, and loved. He brought shalom to the lost sheep. It is this Jesus, this same Jesus who comes again to us in the Resurrection. Jesus does not change.

Some get it wrong not because they believe in judgment; judgment is shot through the resurrection gospel message. Judgment is misinterpreted by those who perceive final judgment as penal or retributive. They have a way of sugar coating how it is that God could be gracious incarnate in Jesus but still retributive in fury at the End of All Things. Grace, blessing, shalom: these are all temporal, for a certain period of time, so they say. As such, these virtues or attributes do not reflect the heart of God. This is what is known in theology as the Augustinian "hidden God" concept. To assert there is a God who acts other than how Jesus acted (in the consistency of life, death and resurrection) is to say exactly what people who live in fear say. There is a reason to fear this kind of a god. But it was the love of God, announced as "shalom" that exorcised all the fear demons ("perfect love casts out fear") from the disciples. It washes away our fear as well. The resurrection gospel is God's message, God's method of interpretation and God's reality. There is no fear in following the God of the resurrected Jesus.

Jesus invites us to choose the God and caregiver of Israel, maker of heaven and earth. We are turned specifically to a merciful and compassionate caregiver ("Abba"). It is this God that we encounter in the resurrection, not some hidden deity, who has a hidden grudge against us. The eschatology of most second-Temple Judaism and much of Christendom is rather bleak and forecasts a great time of trial and a bitter war with a very bloody end and worse—heavenly threat. Most eschatological figures in second Temple literature—and Jesus in some Christian literature, art, and music—come back with a sword or a war. This is a torturous view of Jesus, horrid and dead wrong.[4]

Just before the crucifixion, an event occurs in which Jesus makes clear that a second Temple Jewish eschatological ending was possible. After Peter draws his sword and attacks one of the arresting parties in Gethsemane, Jesus has to tell Peter that violence is not the way. Jesus affirms this by saying he could, if he so chose, call legions of holy angels and start an apocalyptic bloodbath. That, however, is not the way of the Abba. The sword is not, cannot, and never will be the answer. Jesus renounces violence, including apocalyptic violence at that point. This was already

4. Stephen Finamore, *God, Order, and Chaos* reads the Apocalypse of John through a mimetic theoretical lens and validates the major studies of Bauckham, Aune, Grimsrud, Johns, and others that the christological control of the Apocalypse is the lamb Christology.

prefigured in the temptation narratives of Matthew and Luke who have Jesus being offered the entire planet if he would just give glory to the satanic principle of sacred violence. In his resurrection, Jesus comes as the renouncer of apocalyptic vengeance, which is the realm of the "satanically inspired old age." Jesus' message is one of Shalom.

If I may riff for a moment on Schwager's dramatic theology,[5] the resurrection, the first act of the future, is followed by a second act, the ascension, and a third act, the sending of the Holy Spirit. Everything that happened between Easter morning and Pentecost is all part of the same eschatological reality. The Risen Jesus is the Herald of all that is coming. Matthew, Mark, Luke, and John all make these connections. Matthew ends with a commissioning, his version of Pentecost, John has the sending of the Spirit occur in the crucifixion of Jesus and mention of an ascension, and Luke, of course, speaks of all three in Luke 24 and Acts 1–2. However, even earlier than this is the text known as the hymn of Philippians 2:5–11. Assuming an early-50s CE date for the letter, it is probable that the hymn fragment quoted in Phil 2:5–11 is older. Some have posited an Aramaic original underlying the Greek text which takes it all the way back to the Aramaic-speaking churches in the Holy Land. This kind of thinking could be very early and may well constitute evidence for an early core confession of faith.[6]

In Phil 2:5–11, the resurrection of Jesus climaxes the compressed narrative of incarnation, life, and death. The resurrection stanza references the ascension as an end process. Jesus may start "in the clouds" in Luke, but he

5. Schwager, *Jesus in the Drama of Salvation.*

6. See Gathercole, *Pre-existent Son* for this case in the Synoptic Gospels.

ends up at the right hand of the Majesty on High. There he is given the greatest mystery of all. He is given The Name. The unpronounceable Name. The Name of God. He is named The Name. Now, The Name is given a name, the name of Jesus. The unpronounceable is pronounceable, and that pronouncement is good news, no, it is great news for us all! God, in the very depths of God's own heart, loves us with an immense love. Love honored love when Jesus was given The Name.

The exaltation of Jesus to the right hand of the One he knew as "Abba" is one of the most important elements of the resurrection gospel. The most oft-cited text from the Jewish Scriptures in the New Testament is Ps 110:1, a text cited to demonstrate the exaltation of Jesus to the right Hand of Majesty. Whether through *hymnody* ("worship") or *florilegia* ("collections of biblical texts"), early on in their life, the earliest Christians through Ps 110:1 connected the Easter events as one: resurrection, ascension and sending of the Spirit.

What is the significance of the ascension for the Easter message? The ascension affirms God's love for the human species and through the human, all creation, when it is a human that is seated and given The Name above all names. It is the affirmation, however, of a very specific type of human, the True Human, a true son of the Abba. From this point on Jesus alone is the true model for humans of who God is and what God is like just as he is our model for who we may and can be. The enthronement of Jesus is not generic but quite specific; it is the valorization of a life lived completely devoted to seeking and doing the will of the Abba. At the heart of that will or reign was that God does not operate with an economy of exchange; that Abba was gracious, merciful, loving and compassionate; and that deeper still, Abba was all forgiving and non-retaliatory.

In other words, the event of the crucifixion has left its stamp upon everything including the Risen Christ who is the model, the True Human model for Christian believers, and the Spirit who is sent from the Father as "another" (*allos* not *heteros*) *paraclete*. The intimate correlation of the death of Jesus and the giving of the Spirit in the Fourth Gospel, its cruciform pneumatology is well known among Johannine scholars. Less well known is that the same christological understanding underlies both the Johannine Jesus and that of the hymn of Phil 2:5–11 and can also be found in the sermon to the Hebrews. The Johannine Jesus gives his life freely of himself, the Hymned Christ "emptied himself by not grasping," and the Christ of Hebrews "offers himself." The same thing could be said for Jesus' saying in Mark 10:45 where the allusive, if not illusive "Son of Man came to offer his life a ransom for many."

Here the implications of a non-sacrificial view of the atonement are brought to earth. On the cross, Jesus is a model of what it means to be a forgiving victim. In his aforementioned essay, LeRon Shults brings Abelard's moral theory of atonement into conversation with mimetic theory. His conclusion is not only that mimetic theory—particularly mediated desire—play an important role in atonement theory, he also is able to show that the older distinctions between "subjective" and "objective" in which the "subjective" is regarded perjoratively no longer hold. Furthermore, his analysis leads him to ask very serious and important questions with real world consequences. In other words, atonement has to do with ethics.

As Shults avers,

> In this context, I have focused on the ways in which developments within the new sciences of morality can contribute toward a theological reconceptualization of the dynamics that make love real, that make us at-one, binding us in healthy ways to proximate others and to the ultimate sacred Other beyond our control, which Christians experience as divine grace. Is the violence of divine warfare or legalized torture the only way for us to experience reconciliation? For God's sake, I hope not. For goodness sake, I hope we can participate in the prosocial emotional contagion empathically manifested in the salubrious exemplarity of Jesus of Nazareth, among others.

When I travel, I have a certain presentation I use that contains a slide with a quote from a friend of mine. It is brilliant for its demonstration of the connection between atonement and ethics and the problem of seeing the cross as a place where human suffering is valorized. My friend John Stoner said,

> Any atonement theology, dealing with the cross as it does, must be able to make a credible interpretation of Jesus' words in Mark 8:34: "He called the crowd with his disciples, and said to them, 'If any want to become my followers, let them deny themselves and take up their cross, and follow me.'" In other words, a credible description of the meaning of the cross for the followers of Jesus is not adiaphora. Indeed, why should this not be equally important with our certainties about the meaning of Jesus' cross,

since Jesus himself left no room for the disciple
to avoid his or her own cross?[7]

However, if we are asking what concretely does this
discipleship entail, it means not only transitioning from a
mythic victim to the innocent but retributive victim, but
it also means intentionally choosing to become a forgiving person in all relationships. This does not mean being
a doormat or remaining in abusive relationships. It does
mean that in the body of Christ we are constantly practic-
ing this forgiveness with one another. When we repent
and believe the gospel—the good news that God's Final
Solution to the human problem of violence is not a violent
one—we can give ourselves permission to stop demanding payback for where we have been wronged. Until we
believe this news about God the practice of forgiveness
will feel wrong to us precisely because it feels ungodly. Jesus' ethics are not general ethics but specifically for those
called to be followers of his path—a path which is devi-
ant and ungodly if God's justice is vengeance instead of
forgiveness. Living *sub theologia crucis* is living in relation
to all others as a forgiving victim. What does this positive
mimesis, this following of the Risen Lord Jesus look like?

In the early church positive mimesis had a specific
form known as *didache* or "teaching." Aaron Milevec in
his commentary on the document known as *The Didache*
makes a convincing case that early Christian catechesis
involved a) a mentoring relationship, b) time, between
one and three years, and c) a tradition that was memo-
rized. It was the practice of this particular tradition for

7. From an email of January 2, 2007, cited in Hardin, *Stricken
by God?*, 72.

a season that brought the candidate to baptism and thus inclusion into the ecclesia.[8]

We can detect this tradition in three different sources: Matthew's Sermon on the Mount, Luke's Sermon on the Plain, and The Didache. The form is that of the Jewish *derek eresh*, two ways or paths. Each of these three apostolic documents stress the positive relational qualities of mercy, compassion and forgiveness. In The Didache this is grounded in the very first thing a novitiate learns: the great commandment. Early Christians understood that this new way of living had deep social and political implications; one could, in theory, lose one's head over it or get crucified upside down. Love came with a cost. Dietrich Bonhoeffer could observe the difference between "cheap grace" and "costly grace" in 1937, and would say that when "Christ calls a person, he bids them come and die." Love costs the lover. This is the first thing a novitiate learns to practice. This is what used to be called a *habitus*, an interior posture, the way one sets one's intention to live.

I am aware of only a few contemporary Protestant interpretations of spirituality from a mimetic perspective. Abbot Andrew Marr of Three Rivers Monastery articulates a mimetic reading of the Rule of St. Benedict.[9] Overall, it is a brilliant exposition on how mimetic theory and the Benedictine Rule share many common insights and what this means concretely in relationships with a monastic community. I highly recommend it even if one does not live in monastic community.

Vern Redekop has explored similar dynamics of community orientation in *From Violence to Blessing*. Unlike Marr, who focuses on a very specific branch of a

8. Milevec, *The Didache*.
9. Marr, *Tools for Peace*.

specific type of Christianity, Redekop looks at spirituality through the dynamics of First Nations medicine traditions generating a relational mimesis of mutual blessing. Blessing is generated by generosity or hospitality and the acknowledgement of grace or thanksgiving. Blessing is a relationship of transparency and vulnerability. Marr would absolutely concur with this, as do I.

At Preaching Peace, I have taken a slightly different track. In 2002, my family and I began learning nature observation and tracking in an Apache tradition. Since 2004, we have participated in the medicine journey. I went into this as a true and total skeptic and tell the story of how I learned to integrate mimetic theory, Christian theology, and native shamanism in my autobiographical *Walking with Grandfather*. Ecospirituality is, or can be, a positive practice, particularly as it relates to becoming whole as a human. Preaching Peace shares this discovery process of connecting with the creation, God and the other in its week-long Making Peace events.[10] Each of us three mimetic theorists have been able to fruitfully use the mimetic anthropology and unpack how Christian formation is practiced and especially how the cruciform character of that formation (that is, in full cognizance of the scapegoat mechanism), that *habitus*, plays itself out in social relations. Ethics and spirituality—like theology, christology, pneumatology, ecclesiology, soteriology, and eschatology—are all framed *sub theologia crucis* where the revelation of God reconciling the world took place.

Marr, Redekop, and I all share in common that because we affirm the *interdividual* character of the human, we can correlate spirituality with community and the healing, restoring and nurturing of relationships. All

10. Information can be found at www.preachingpeace.org.

three of us have been informed by the seismic epistemological shift to relationality in the twentieth century. Because of this all three of us are able to correlate ethics and spirituality; the dynamics of both are one and the same. It all comes down to one thing. It is so simple that it defies belief. I am certain if I tell you, you will think I have gone bonkers.

The text I have cited several times now, Phil 2:5–11, gets right to the heart of the "how" of this spirituality and ethics. In nineteenth century discussion this text was used as the basis for a discussion around Jesus kenotic self-emptying. How did Jesus do this? Much ink was spilled parsing natures and attributes all in attempt to figure the "how." Yet it is the "how" that is enjoined by Paul that is to be imitated: "Have this mind in you which also was in Christ Jesus . . ."

A fuller study of this text is able to show that the Adam-Christ typology correlates soteriology and ethics through the allusion to mimetic grasping.

Adam (Genesis 1–3)	Christ (Phil 2:5–11)
Made in divine image	Being the image of God
thought it a prize to	thought it not a prize to
grasp at to be as God;	grasp at to be as God;
and aspired to a reputation	and made himself of no reputation
And spurned being God's	And took upon himself the form
servant	of a servant

Adam (Genesis 1–3)	Christ (Phil 2:5–11)
seeking to be in the likeness	and was made in the likeness of
of God;	humanity
and being found in fashion as	and being found in fashion as
a man (of dust, now doomed)	a human
He exalted himself	He humbled himself
and became disobedient	and became obedient
unto death.	unto death
He was condemned &	God highly exalted Him & gave
disgraced	him The Name and rank of Lord

The difference between Adam and Christ has to do with that fundamental reality that is nonconscious to us: mediated desire. Adam imitated Eve and grasped, and the whole thing spiraled into murder, sacrifice, vengeance, and violence. Jesus does not grasp but *ekenosen*, which we translate as "emptied himself." In light of a mimetic approach it would be appropriate to translate *ekenosen* as "let go," which is the opposite of grasping.[11] This is the principle of discipleship that underlies both Christian ethics and Christian spirituality, as well as Buddhist and aboriginal spirituality. This is the first thing a disciple learns, for it is only letting go that one is able to receive. In *The Jesus Driven Life* I used the term "surrender" to describe

11. A fuller discussion of this text can be found in *The Jesus Driven Life*.

this manner of existence. There is much more that could be said on the psychology of the spiritual journey from a mimetic perspective that would be valuable, but would take us a bit far afield. Suffice it to say that it is possible to develop the framework of a holistic theological-ethical-spiritual approach to the Christian life from a peacemaking perspective informed by the mimetic theory.

We conclude our exploration of mimetic theory by coming back to the beginning: to ritual. If Girard is correct that ritual has a generative priority over prohibition and myth, and it is the ritualizing process that generates religion, then to end by discussing Christian ritual might enervate Christian communities everywhere. In fact, the congruence between liturgy, theology, ethics, and spirituality is astonishing. I believe it is a way of framing the Eucharist *sub theologia crucis* in a non-violent or non-sacrificial manner consistent with our hermeneutic and our ethic. Let's have some fun and start with a little bit of shock and awe, shall we?

> Steve Berry: Clergy don't teach that very frequently. In other words, when they get up and they recite the words of institution, "This is my body, this is my blood. . . . Do this in remembrance of me," it isn't explained to the people who are taking the bread and the cup that this means the end of violence.
>
> René Girard: It means the end of violence, yet at the same time it shows the continuity with a whole history of religion. So when anthropologists tell you, "Hey, that's cannibalism," you should answer, "Yes, of course, cannibalism is part of human history and the Eucharist summarizes it all in nonviolence." Therefore, why not cannibalism there as well? Cannibalism is the essence of sacrifice. Cannibalism

means you eat the sacrificial victim in order
to be your victim, because you want to be that
victim. The reason you killed him is you want
to be him or her. So if you absorb his or her
flesh, you become them, just as if you absorb
the flesh of Christ, you should become a little
bit nonviolent, more than you were before.[12]

Jesus as our sacrifice (after all we are the ones who
"break the bread"), allows us to transfer our hostility to
him as an innocent victim, as a firstborn male or virgin
girl. We kill him. And yes, there is a benefit. His shed
blood becomes our drink, blood shed for our forgiveness.
In his death there is only forgiveness. There is no wrath
from God here; there is only our human wrath, our need
for sacrifice. This is why it is so important to recognize
that when we share the Eucharist we are participating
in the oldest human ritual in the world: primitive sacrifice. But it is a ritual that has now been transcended and
morphed into a communion meal where we no longer
need sacrifice, a meal wherein we no longer need scapegoats, a meal whereby we acknowledge our corporate
propensity to hurt others and expel others in order to create our "in group." In this meal, we acknowledge this by
"breaking bread," and we are also forgiven as we drink the
cup. This is good news, news far better than the archaic
religious practices of violent human culture. The Eucharist, therefore, is the most anti-cultural institution in the
world and breaks down our sacrificial religion and turns
us to a non-sacrificial spirituality where God is love and
where we learn to love one another.

No matter whether your liturgy is maximalist or
minimalist, whether you hold to a "real presence" or a

12. Hardin, *Reading the Bible*, 115.

symbolic presence, the real question about what is occurring in the celebration of this meal of bread and wine need not elude us. It has to do with our fundamental human condition. *The Eucharist addresses our need to kill.*

When the Roman Catholic church speaks of the "sacrifice" of the Eucharist, this does not mean that they believe the priest is re-sacrificing Jesus on the altar. It is the recognition that the act of breaking the bread is analogous to the breaking of the body of Jesus on the cross. That is, just as Jesus' persecutors broke his body, so when we celebrate the Eucharist we acknowledge that we are human "body breakers." When we eat this bread, we confess we are cannibalistic; that is, we seek to consume the "being" of the victim and thus enhance our own "being." The writer of the Fourth Gospel explicitly uses the word "to munch" (*trogein*) in John 6 to bring to mind that this is more than a simple ingestion of food. The use of *trogein* ought to bring to mind sucking the marrow out of bones, of the way we suck life out of one another. In this sense we are all vampiric and the Eucharist is the ritual whereby we acknowledge our social vampirism.

In breaking the bread we confess we are all persecutors, that had we been there, we would have crucified Jesus. *We do not come to this meal with clean hands and pure hearts. We come to it frothing at the mouth, demanding a sacrifice that will take away our personal and social angst, violence, and fear.* We break bread; we confess we are murderers. This is the point. We are the mob, or in religious language, we are all sinners. The proof in the pudding is that we treat the outcast, the marginalized, or the "other" this very way. We do not see Jesus in them. If we did, we would be kind, generous, helpful, and compassionate to them. But we do not see Jesus in them; we are just like the goats in the parable (Matthew 25). When we break the bread we participate in a ritual as old as human religion and culture—the sacrifice of an innocent other. Jesus is our victim. We killed him, each of us participating, all of us together. Scapegoating others has always been our means of redemption, of participating in human community. This is not the end of the story, however, for this ritual has another part—a redemptive part. It is not found in the killing but in the voice of the victim. It is the cup we drink.

In the Eucharist, we come as a killing mob, breaking our victims in order to consume them, to suck the life-force out of them. This is why victims were eventually divinized or made into gods: we sought divine and eternal life in our victims, life beyond death. In our victims we thought we found the answer to our questions. In their death we sought life; in the darkness we brought upon them we sought light. Little did we know that the light within us was a great darkness and that the violence we used against our victims could and would one day turn against us.

So, in breaking the bread, we confess we are murderers. We ignore Jesus as the goats ignore the marginalized. Better they should die than be a drain on our culture. Like the religious and political authorities did to Jesus, we demonize our victims so that in disposing of them we need not feel guilty. Yet, we are most guilty.

Had Jesus been like many victims (or victims' families) he would have sought revenge. How many times have you read in a news report about someone being killed and the family calling for justice? How many times have you read or heard others say that someone who committed a criminal act "got what they deserved?" Retaliation, eye for eye, *lex talionis*, is the way we humans do justice. This is the voice of Abel crying out from the ground for vengeance. "Cain bombed my city and killed innocent me, O God, now kill him to balance the books of the universe." We hear this voice in many of the Psalms where the singer, who is persecuted, cries out for revenge.

Yet, when we take the cup to drink the blood of our Victim, Jesus, Son of God, True Human, Lord of the Universe, is it revenge we hear? No, it is the cup of forgiveness. In his blood we find only forgiveness. There is no hint of revenge either now or in the future. All revenge or retaliation by God is forever forsworn. As the writer to Hebrews says, "Jesus' blood speaks a better word than that of Abel's." Jesus blood does not cry out for justice, his blood cries out for mercy. The one who taught that we ought to "bless those who persecute us" does indeed bless us with forgiveness when we acknowledge our scapegoating ways and when we, in drinking the cup, refuse to be retaliators when we have been wronged. This cup of forgiveness is not just a cup whereby we walk away feeling better and then complain about others or remember our grudges against others. When we put this cup to our lips, we are not only forgiven for what we have done to others but we also acknowledge that others who have hurt us are forgiven as well. God treats us all alike as forgiven murderers. When we drink this cup we drink forgiveness to the dregs and that forgiveness pours out of our life to others. The one who shares in this meal has no enemies. If one walks away from this meal and still holds a grudge or is unwilling to forgive, then, and only then, do they "drink and eat damnation to themselves" for they are not willing to do as Jesus did and leave transgressions behind.

We have all been victims. In the late twentieth century being a victim has become a status symbol. It is *much* harder to recognize that *we are all killers, murderers with our words, thoughts and actions* against those we have deemed "other" or sinful or less worthy than ourselves. This is why we first break the bread and then secondly, drink the cup. It is not the other way around. The Eucharist meets our deepest needs. It meets us in the darkest places in our souls, the place where we would consign "the other" to an eternal hellfire or a life of hell. It liberates all of our victims from the hell we put them in. It calls us to recognize that "with the measure we judge others, we judge ourselves."

I have come to the conclusion that *Protestantism is stuck when it comes to the Eucharist because it has turned the Lord's Supper into a purely symbolic act emptied of its meaning and power*. For most folks a symbol "represents" but is not the thing itself. In so doing, we have dislocated the "real" from the "phenomenal" and the objective from the subjective.

Now I can understand why the Reformers contended against medieval concepts of sacrifice and the Eucharist. Some of Calvin's arguments are quite valid. But something is also missing that I think would help Protestants reinvigorate this precious ritual. That missing piece is the "real presence." By this I don't mean "real presence" in the old categories of metaphysics, where we try to figure out the relation of the visible to the invisible, the spiritual to the material, etc. *By "real presence" I am referring to us, the worshippers*. We are no longer bringing our real selves to the table and thus we are not able to discern the Lord Jesus' "real presence."

When we come to the table we are not bringing our true selves. We have been taught that we must bring our "holy" selves. In fear of some kind of punishment if we are found "eating of the Lord's table in an unworthy manner," we have turned this meal into that which it was never meant to be. We have turned it on its head. The problem in Corinth was the failure to "discern the body" and for Paul the body that he speaks about is the body of Christ, the people. Paul is referring to the sociological problem of the agape meal/Eucharist where the rich had plenty of food while the poor went away hungry. Paul is speaking to the problem of a community which is hierarchical, which had valued persons based upon socio-economic status.

The Eucharist is the one meal where we are all leveled. In this meal we all come as sinners. I don't simply mean that we have committed "sins" and thus have an "I am a sinner, woe is me" mentality. Rather when we come to this meal we are coming to the Passion narrative. We are enacting the crucifixion of Jesus. We are "re-presenting" the arrest, trial, torture and execution of Jesus. We are invited to recognize our solidarity with the mob. In this meal all we need to do to achieve this is to look at the ways in which we have scapegoated others through gossip, spreading falsehoods about another, or genuinely participated in conversations where we have been discriminatory. In short, we are invited to examine the ways we still continue to structure ourselves hierarchically.

This meal breaks down all illusions of good and bad, sin and holiness. In this meal we are all going to get our hands bloody. We are those who would scapegoat the "other" who is different, we seek our differentiation in the "other." The process of "removing" sin is antithetical to this meal for this meal is all about sin; in fact, one might be so bold to say that it is the ultimate act of sin in which we shall ever participate for in this meal we are standing there as the mob that rejects Jesus, that falsely accuses him, that blasphemes against him and we are the ones who drive the nails into his hands and feet. The old spiritual "Were you there when they crucified my Lord?" must be answered in the positive when we come forward to share in this meal, for that is exactly what we are doing by participating in it. The Eucharist is Good Friday over and over again, a ritual intended to drive something home, to drive something so deep into our the fabric of our being that we cannot remain unchanged. That something is all the blood on our hands from those relationships we have destroyed with our thoughts, our actions, and our words. The Eucharist is not just about *breaking bread*; it is the complete and total recognition that in harming the "other," we are *breaking bad*.

We are the persecutory species, complete with systems of laws and punishments that don't fit the crime. In the Eucharist we recognize and experience the pathos of one who was a victim of a legal system that acted perfectly within its rights, yet even though legal brought injustice. Ours will always be a perversion of justice. Why? *Because we know of no other way as a species to exist except by marginalizing the other*.

This is not to say that other allusions to the Eucharist are not meaningful. Geoffrey Wainwright has shown the overwhelming eschatological themes in the Eucharist in the church fathers.[13] Of course, one could also develop a Eucharistic theology with reference to the Passover. I am simply saying that if Protestants wish to participate in the meal, they first have to acknowledge it as a sacrifice—

13. Wainright, *Eucharist and Eschatology*.

their sacrifice—which means they have to acknowledge an atonement theory where humanity alone is culpable in the death of Jesus. As long as the Eucharist remains sanitized on prettified altars or deformed by a poor understanding of symbols and ritual, the celebration of the Eucharist will be nothing other than a religious celebration of the sacrificial mechanism. Either way works, sanitizing or demoting the ritual.

When we break bread, we are to come as our real selves, as persecutors and prosecutors and finger pointers, those who are quite happy to blame the other. When the priest "breaks the bread" if we do not see ourselves in solidarity with that priest, as our representative, if we fail to see that we are culpable, we will not have any right to share in the cup that follows. For how can we be forgiven if we do not sin? It is not just wheat that is ground up, mixed, kneaded, and baked that we are breaking; we are *breaking bad* with Jesus' flesh. *We are killing him.*

Yes, this meal is tied to the Passover by the Gospel tradition. Yes, this meal is a meal of deliverance, an exodus from our bondage to victimizing others. *But it is only that because it is the oldest social ritual we possess: the act of a community that hunts down and blames a random victim, kills them, and eats them.* We are cannibals. Human culture is at its core cannibalistic culture. We have simply prettied it up with laws and prohibitions, with state sponsored executions, by turning the church into exclusive little country clubs where we dress so fine and mutter under our breath about those who don't look like us, dress like us, or act like us. Our services have become spectacles filled with the latest in multi-media to entertain us, lights and sound that distract us from the real activity that is happening. For what is really happening is gross beyond belief. It is abhorrent to all of our senses. While we think we are worshipping the Lord with our voices raised loud and our hands held high, we have hidden ourselves from the victim who writhes upon the altar, in whose body we will all share, ripping the flesh with our teeth and sucking the marrow from the bones. We do this with eyes wide shut. For we think that we derive life from our victims. We all walk away from this meal with blood on our hands but we are absolutely clueless.

This is why the Jesus of the Fourth Gospel uses such intense language about the Eucharist in John 6 and so intimately ties our feeding on him to the language of cannibalism ("*trogein*"). Yes, we derive life from our victims, but it is *the pseudo life* of the Lie, the Lie that we are just and right in what we do when scapegoating others and creating distinctions between us and them. In Jesus' meal, with its identical structure, we are invited to recall and experience all this, to be "really present" to all this, to thus discern his "real presence" in all this. In so doing, we may also share in him who is a different kind of bread. He is not the bread that brings and justifies death; Jesus is the Bread of Life.

When we eat his flesh, when we gnaw on his bones, we are bringing his life into ourselves (as it were). In so doing we are bringing nonviolence—life-giving, life-affirming nonviolence—right into the core of our very being. When we eat his body, we are not magically ingesting some metaphysical or spiritual reality that is meant to make us feel better about ourselves; we are taking into our deepest being the one who would restore all of our relationships. *The Lord's Supper is not an I-me-my event, it is a communal event given to us to re-create the very way we do community*. It teaches us to be "holy" for it shows us how to be "whole." No more scapegoats. No more differentiating ourselves from others. We are those who, in sharing the body of Christ, are the only community on the planet that practices a victimizing ritual with eyes wide open so that we may be healed and in turn heal others.

DISCUSSION QUESTIONS:

1. How does the author correlate Jesus' eschatological views and second Temple views?

2. What is the truly "new" in the Easter event and announcement?

3. How important is it that Jesus is our model in light of our mimetic existence?

4. What is the role of nonviolence and caregiving in relation to others? In relation to the Earth? In relation to ourselves?

5. How might a mimetic rendering of the Eucharist aid us in our ethics and spirituality?

7

POSTLUDE

THE FOLLOWING BIBLIOGRAPHY CONTAINS reference to all of the major works by René Girard. Significant works by mimetic theorists on biblical and theological topics are also mentioned. There are also many essays that one can find in the bibliography on the website of the Colloquium on Violence and Religion.

In addition to literature, I want to mention a number of organizations that are helping to advance mimetic theory. First, there is Imitatio, a San Francisco-based philanthropic organization dedicated to engaging mimetic theory in the academy. Their website contains a catalogue of books underwritten with Michigan State University Press, including the translations of Girard's *When These Things Begin* and *The One by Whom Scandal Comes*. William Johnsen has done a stellar job of bringing more than a score of excellent books to press. In addition to containing information on these publications, many of Girard's own works can be read freely on the Imitatio website. It has been an honor to work with the executive leadership of Imitatio and to be a beneficiary of the generosity of Mr. Peter Thiel.

Second, I must mention Raven Foundation, an organization co-founded by Keith and Suzanne Ross. Raven bloggers and writers examine contemporary American culture and world events. The Raven Foundation sponsors a number of millennial thinkers and platforms who use mimetic theory to understand current theological issues and the arts. Suzanne reads the story of the wicked witch of the West—as her story is told in the theatrical production *Wicked*—through the lens of Girard's scapegoat mechanism, and the play's powerful and subversive overtones are brought to light. Their website contains links to blogs, lectures, and cultural events related to mimetic theory.

James Warren is a world-class magician. James has a magic show he gives in public schools as it relates to the problem of bullying and the solution of peacemaking. He has created an excellent day-long seminar combining magic with mimetic theory. His book *Compassion or Apocalypse* is my current favorite book to recommend to the literate inquirer. Paul Neuchterlein has been running the website www.girardianlectionary.net for twenty years and now enjoys teaching mimetic theory and Christian formation. Contact both James and Paul if your church or school is seeking knowledgeable and entertaining speakers.

Anthony and Linda Bartlett, in Syracuse, New York, are living out what a positive mimetic vision looks like in communities like Wood Hath Hope and Bethany House. Tony is one of the most stimulating thinkers at the intersection of mimetic theory and Christian theology. Andrew

Marr, abbot of an Episcopalian Benedictine Monastery in Three Rivers, Michigan, lives out this same positive mimetic vision in a liturgical context. Both are excellent examples of how a positive mimetic community is formed and maintained.

Finally, the Colloquium on Violence and Religion sponsors the annual "Girardian" meeting of scholars from many disciplines and backgrounds. Membership fees are quite low and the benefits are many. COV&R is an affiliate group of the American Academy of Religion. Their website contains information on upcoming meetings as well as a bibliographic database (not exhaustive) of articles and books engaging the mimetic theory.

Videos, podcasts, essays, and e-books engaging mimetic theory can be found on our website at www.preachingpeace.org. There is also information on my speaking itinerary and The School of Peace Theology.

BIBLIOGRAPHY

Alison, James. *The Joy of Being Wrong: Original Sin through Easter Eyes*. New York: Crossroad, 1998.

Antonello, Pierpaolo, and Paul Gifford, eds. *Can We Survive Our Origins?* East Lansing: Michigan State University Press, 2015.

———. *How We Became Human: Mimetic Theory and the Science of Evolutionary Origins*. East Lansing: Michigan State University Press, 2015.

Astell, Ann, and Sandor Goodhart. *Sacrifice, Scripture & Substitution*. Notre Dame: University of Notre Dame Press, 2011.

Bailie, Gil. *Violence Unveiled: Humanity at the Crossroads*. New York: Crossroad, 1995.

Baker, Sharon. *Razing Hell*. Philadelphia: Westminster John Knox, 2010.

Bandera, Cesáreo. *A Refuge of Lies: Reflections on Faith and Fiction* East Lansing: Michigan State University Press, 2013.

———. *The Sacred Game: The Role of the Sacred in the Genesis of Modern Literary Fiction*. University Park: Penn State University Press, 1996.

Bartlett, Anthony. *Cross Purposes*. Harrisburg, PA: Trinity, 2001.

———. *Virtually Christian: How Christ Changed Human Meaning and Makes Creation New*. Washington DC: O-Books, 2011.

Bauckham, Richard. *Jesus and the God of Israel*. Grand Rapids: Eerdmans, 2008.

Bibliography

Bernstein, Alan. *The Formation of Hell*. London: UCL Press, 1993.

Campbell, Douglas. *The Deliverance of God*. Grand Rapids: Eerdmans, 2009.

————. *Framing Paul: An Epistolary Biography*. Grand Rapids: Eerdmans, 2014.

Cowdell, Scott. *Abiding Faith: Christianity Beyond Certainty, Anxiety and Violence*. Eugene: Cascade, 2009.

————. *René Girard and Secular Modernity: Christ, Culture, and Crisis*. South Bend, IN: University of Notre Dame Press, 2013.

Cowdell, Scott, Joel Hodge, and Chris Fleming, eds. *Violence, Desire, and the Sacred*. Vol 1. New York: Continuum, 2012.

————. *Violence, Desire, and the Sacred*. Vol 2. New York: Continuum, 2014.

Depoortere, Frederick. *Christ in Postmodern Philosophy: Gianni Vattimo, René Girard and Slavoj Žižek*. Edinburgh: T. & T. Clark, 2008.

Dumochel, Paul, ed. *Violence and Truth*. Stanford: Stanford University Press, 1988.

Dupuy, Jean-Pierre. *The Mark of the Sacred*. East Lansing: Michigan State University Press, 2013.

Finamore, Stephen. *God, Order, and Chaos: René Girard and the Apocalypse*. Eugene: Wipf & Stock, 2009.

Fishbane, Michael. *Biblical Interpretation in Ancient Israel*. Oxford: Clarendon, 1985.

Fleming, Chris. *René Girard: Violence and Mimesis*. Malden: Polity, 2004.

Garrels, Scott R., ed. *Mimesis and Science: Empirical Research on Imitation and the Mimetic Theory of Culture and Religion*. East Lansing, MI: Michigan State University Press, 2011.

Gathercole, Simon. *The Pre-existent Son: Recovering the Christologies of Matthew, Mark and Luke*. Grand Rapids: Eerdmans, 2006.

Girard, René. *Achever Clausewitz (Battling to the End)*. Translated by Mary Baker. East Lansing: Michigan State University Press, 2010.

————. "The Ancient Trail Trodden by the Wicked." *Semeia* 33 (1985) 13–42.

————. *Celui par qui le scandale arrive (The One by Whom Scandal Comes)*. Translated by M. B. DeBevoise. East Lansing: Michigan State University Press, 2014.

————. *Critique dans un souterrain*. Translated by James. G. Williams. East Lansing: Michigan State University Press, 2012.

———. *Des choses cachées depuis la foundation du monde* (*Things Hidden from the Foundation of the World*). Translated by Stephen Bann and Michael Metteer. Stanford: Stanford University Press, 1987.

———. *De La Violence à La Divinite*. Paris: Grasset et Fasquelle, 2007.

———. *Evolution and Conversion: Dialogues on the Origins of Culture*. London: T. & T. Clark, 2007.

———. "The Evangelical Subversion of Myth." In *Politics and Apocalypse*, edited by Robert G. Hamerton-Kelly, 29–50. East Lansing, MI: Michigan State University Press, 2007.

———. "Generative Scapegoating." In *Violent Origins: Ritual Killing and Cultural Formation,* edited by Robert G. Hamerton-Kelly, 73–148. Stanford: Stanford University Press, 1987.

———. "Interview with Christian anthropologist René Girard" by Hervé Morin. *Le Monde des livres*, 5 Oct., 2009.

———. *Je vois satan tomber comme l'éclair* (*I See Satan Fall Like Lightning*). Translated by James G. Williams. Maryknoll: Orbis, 2001.

———. *La route antique des homes pervers* (*Job: The Victim of His People*). Translated by Yvonne Freccero. Stanford: Stanford University Press, 1985.

———. *La violence et le sacré* (*Violence and the Sacred*). Translated by Patrick Henry. Baltimore: Johns Hopkins, 1977.

———. *Le bouc émissaire* (*The Scapegoat*). Translated by Yvonne Freccero. Paris: Grasset et Fasquelle, 1982.

———. *Le sacrifice (Sacrifice)*. Translated by David Dawson and Matthew Pattillo. East Lansing: Michigan State University Press, 2011.

———. *Mensonge romantique et vérité romanesque (Deceit, Desire, and the Novel)*. Translated by Yvonne Freccero. Baltimore: Johns Hopkins, 1965.

———. *Mimesis and Theory*. Edited by Robert Doran. Stanford: Stanford University Press, 2008.

———. "Mimetische Theorie und Theologie." In *Von Fluch und Segen der Sündenböcke,* edited by Józef Niewiasdomki and Wolfgang Palaver. Thaur: Kulturverlag, 1995.

———. *Oedipus Unbound: Selected Writings on Rivalry and Desire*. Edited by Mark Anspach. Stanford: Stanford University Press, 2004.

Bibliography

———. *Quand ces choses commenceront (When These Things Begin)*. Translated by Trevor Cribben Merrill. East Lansing: Michigan State University Press, 2014.

———. "Simone Weil vue par René Girard." *Cahiers* 9.3.

———. *A Theater of Envy*. New York: Oxford University Press, 1991.

———. *To Double Business Bound*. Baltimore: Johns Hopkins University Press, 1978.

Girard, René, and Gianni Vattimo. *Christianity, Truth, and Weakening Faith: A Dialogue*. New York: Columbia University Press, 2003.

Golson, Richard J. *René Girard and Myth*. New York: Routledge, 2002.

Goodhart, Sandor. *Sacrificing Commentary: Reading the End of Literature*. Baltimore: Johns Hopkins, 1996.

Goodhart, Sandor, et al., eds. *For René Girard: Essays in Friendship and Truth*. East Lansing: Michigan State University Press, 2009.

Grande, Per Bjorner. *Girard's Christology*. Online: www.preaching peace.org.

———. *Mimesis and Desire: An Analysis of the Religious Nature of Mimesis and Desire in the Work of René Girard*. Saarbrücken, Germany: Lambert Academic, 2009.

Grote, Jim, and John McGeeney. *Clever as Serpents: Business Ethics and Office Politics*. Collegeville: Liturgical, 1997.

Hamerton-Kelly, Robert G. *The Gospel and the Sacred: Poetics of Violence in Mark*. Minneapolis: Fortress, 1994.

———. *Sacred Violence: Paul's Hermeneutic of the Cross*. Minneapolis: Fortress, 1992.

———. "An Introductory Essay." In *Politics and Apocalypse,* edited by Robert Hamerton-Kelly, 1–28. East Lansing, MI: Michigan State University Press, 2007.

Hardin, Michael. "American Protestant Reception of Girard." In *Handbook on Mimetic Theory* (forthcoming).

———. *The Jesus Driven Life*. 2nd ed. Lancaster, PA: JDL Press, 2013.

———. "Mimesis and Dominion: The Dynamics of Violence and the Imitation of Christ in Maximus Confessor." *St Vladimir's Theological Quarterly* 36.4 (1992) 373–86.

———. "Mimetic Theory & Christian Theology in the 21st Century." In *For René Girard: Essays in Friendship and Truth,* edited by Sandor Goodhart et al., 265–72. East Lansing: Michigan State University Press, 2009.

———. *Must God Be Violent?: Religion and Revelation in Karl Barth and René Girard*. PhD diss., Charles Sturt University, 2017.

Bibliography

———. "Practical Implications of Nonviolent Atonement." In *Violence, Desire, and the Sacred,* vol 2, edited by Scott Cowdell, Joel Hodge, and Chris Fleming, 247–58. New York: Continuum, 2014.

———, ed. *Reading the Bible with René Girard: Conversations with Steven E. Berry.* Lancaster: JDL Press, 2015.

———. "Sacrificial Language in the 'Letter to the Hebrews.'" In *Violence Renounced,* edited by Willard Swartley, 103–19. Telford, PA: Pandora, 2000.

———. "Violence: René Girard and the Recovery of Early Christian Perspectives." *Brethren Life and Thought* 37.2 (1992) 107–20.

———. *Walking with Grandfather.* Lancaster, PA: JDL Press, 2013.

———. *What the Facebook? Posts from the Edge of Christendom* Vol. 1–3. Lancaster, PA: JDL Press, 2014–2016.

Hardin, Michael, and Brad Jersak. *Stricken by God? Nonviolent Identification and the Victory of Christ.* Grand Rapids: Eerdmans, 2007.

Hardin, Michael, and Ted Grimsrud. *Compassionate Eschatology.* Eugene: Cascade, 2011.

Heim, S. Mark. *Saved from Sacrifice: A Theology of the Cross.* Grand Rapids: Eerdmans, 2006.

Jersak, Brad. *Her Gates Will Never Be Shut.* Eugene: Wipf & Stock, 2009.

Juilland, Alphonse, ed. *To Honor René Girard.* Stanford: Anma Libri, 1986.

Kirwan, Michael. *Girard and Theology.* Edinburgh: T. & T. Clark, 2009.

König, Adrio. *The Eclipse of Christ in Eschatology: Toward a Christ-Centered Approach.* Grand Rapids: Eerdmans, 1989.

Kugel, James L., and Rowan A. Greer. *Early Biblical Interpretation.* Philadelphia: Westminster, 1986.

Kümmel, Werner Georg. *The New Testament: The History of the Investigation of its Problems.* Nashville: Abingdon, 1970.

Livingston, Paisley. *Models of Desire: René Girard and the Psychology of Mimesis.* Baltimore: Johns Hopkins, 1992.

Mack, Burton. *The Myth of Innocence: Mark and Christian Origins.* Philadelphia: Fortress, 1988.

Marr, Andrew. *Tools for Peace: The Spiritual Craft of St. Benedict and René Girard.* New York: iUniverse, 2007.

Martyn, J. Louis. *Galatians.* New York: Doubleday, 1997.

McKenna, Andrew. "Introduction." *Semeia* 33 (1985) 1–12.

———. *Violence and Difference: Girard, Derrida, and Deconstruction.* Urbana: University of Illinois Press, 1992.

Milavec, Aaron. *The Didache.* New York: Newman, 2003.

Morin, Hervé. "Interview with Christian Anthropologist René Girard" *Le Monde des livres*, October 5, 2009.

Pahl, Jon. *Empire of Sacrifice: The Religious Origins of American Violence.* New York: New York University Press, 2012.

Palaver, Wolfgang. *René Girard's Mimetic Theory.* Translated by Gabriel Borrud. East Lansing: Michigan State University Press, 2013.

Phelan, John E. *Essential Eschatology.* Downers Grove, IL: InterVarsity, 2013.

Redekop, Vern. *From Violence to Blessing: How an Understanding of Deep Rooted Conflict Can Open Paths to Reconciliation.* Ottawa: Novalis, 2002.

Rogerson, John, Christopher Rowland, and Barnabas Lindars. *The Study and Use of the Bible.* Grand Rapids: Eerdmans, 1988.

Russell, Jeffrey Burton. *The Devil.* Ithaca, NY: Cornell University Press, 1977.

———. *Lucifer.* Ithaca, NY: Cornell University Press, 1984.

———. *Mephistopheles.* Ithaca, NY: Cornell University Press, 1986.

———. *The Prince of Darkness.* Ithaca, NY: Cornell University Press, 1988.

———. *Satan.* Ithaca, NY: Cornell University Press, 1981.

Scholder, Klaus. *The Birth of Modern Critical Theory: Origins and Problems of Biblical Criticism in the Seventeenth Century.* Philadelphia: Trinity, 1990.

Shults, LeRon. "Ethics, Exemplarity and Atonement." In *Theology and the Science of Moral Action: Virtue Ethics, Exemplarity, and Cognitive Neuroscience*, edited by James van Slyke, et al., 164–78. London: Routledge, 2012.

———. *The Postfoundationalist Task of Theology.* Grand Rapids: Eerdmans, 1999.

———. *Reforming Theological Anthropology.* Grand Rapids: Eerdmans, 2003.

Schwager, Raymund. "Christ's Death and the Prophetic Critique of Sacrifice." *Semeia* 33 (1985) 109–24.

———. "Der Richter wird gericht: Zur Versöhnungslehre von Karl Barth." In *Der wundebare Tausch*, 232–72. München: Kosel, 1986.

———. *Jesus in the Drama of Salvation.* New York: Crossroad, 1999.

———. *Must There Be Scapegoats?* New York: Harper and Row, 1987.

Scubla, Lucien. "The Christianity of René Girard and the Nature of Religion." In *Violence and Truth*, edited by Paul Dumochel, 160–78. Stanford: Stanford University Press, 1988.

Simonetti, Manilo. *Biblical Interpretation in the Early Church*. Edinburgh: T. & T. Clark, 1994.

Sollers, Philippe. "Is God Dead?" In *To Honor René Girard*, 191–96. Saratoga: ANMA Libri, 1986.

Theissen, Gert. *The Gospels in Context*. Minneapolis: Fortress, 1991.

Tilling, Chris. *Paul's Divine Christology*. Grand Rapids: Eerdmans, 2012.

Wainright, Geoffrey. *Eucharist and Eschatology*. New York: Oxford University Press, 1981.

Webb, Eugene. *Philosophers of Consciousness*. Seattle: University of Washington Press, 1988.

Williams, James G. *The Bible, Violence and the Sacred*. San Francisco: Harper Collins, 1991.

———. *The Girardians*. Zurich: LIT Verlag, 2012.

———, ed. *The Girard Reader*. New York: Crossroad, 1996.

Williams, Rowan. "Girard on Violence, Society and the Sacred." In *Wrestling with Angels*, edited by Mike Higton, 171–85. Grand Rapids: Eerdmans, 2007.